Outlines

MONTGOMERY CLIFT

To my parents and Tadeusz Deręgowski

Outlines

MONTGOMERY CLIFT

DAVID LANCASTER

Absolute Press

First published in 2005 by

Absolute Press
Scarborough House,
29 James Street West,
Bath, England BA1 2BT
Phone 01225 316013
Fax 01225 445836
E-mail outlines@absolutepress.co.uk
Web www.absolutepress.co.uk

Series editor Nick Drake

Printed by Legoprint, Italy

ISBN 1 904573 08 8

Contents

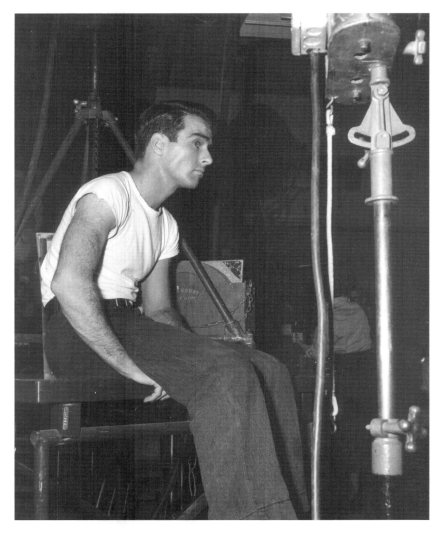

'A QUIZZICAL GHOST, A SHADOW SELF.'
MONTGOMERY CLIFT ON THE SET OF *A PLACE IN THE SUN* IN 1949.

'God Bless the Sunday Matinée'

Sorry I'm a bit husky; the dead aren't used to speaking. But now you're about to begin, I wanted to remind you how we first met, back in the days when the movies first entered your blood and showed you what life was, and what it could be. As your hand hovers over the page, I stand at your shoulder, a quizzical ghost, a shadow self. Remember how I was another, different shadow back then?

I came to you when you were six or so, out of the old black and white television set that presided over your back room like an electronic Buddha. There had been others before me, but they'd all been gargoyles. Sam Jaffe as the wizened High Llama in Lost Horizon, *Martita Hunt as Miss Havisham, alone among the cobwebs of* Great Expectations: *how their age and despair frightened you, how firmly they clamped their hands across your mouth. 'This could be your fate,' the High Llama croaked. 'Here,' whispered Miss Havisham, 'here is the haunted wood, and one day, boy, you'll have to cut your way through.'*

But me, on that long ago Sunday afternoon: I was another matter, wasn't I? Nothing constricted there, just a slender neck, a cut glass profile and some pretty cute Victorian frills. How beautiful I was, especially in the final sequence when I was leaning with my forehead pressed against the door, while, on the other side, in the great house, a crinolined woman retreated upstairs. Thump, thump, thump on the wood; no answer from her receding lamp. Would there be? Would the young woman, who loved me, and who I loved, stir herself and let me in? I guess in that heightened moment you wanted to let me in, to give me free rein among the gargoyles, so I could scatter their dust with one brush of my pretty lips. I offered you the first glimpse of the way through your haunted wood....

You did. I remember.

So God bless those BBC Sunday Matinées.

No, God bless the movies. God bless you.

★

Edward Montgomery Clift (1920-1966) is a compelling figure. At the time he pleaded unsuccessfully with Olivia de Havilland in *The Heiress* (1949), he had already appeared in two acclaimed films − *The Search* (1948) and *Red River* (1948) − and was fast establishing himself as a new breed of star, the first of the 'rebel males' as the cultural critic Graham McCann has called them. During his heyday, which lasted until a devastating car crash wrecked his face and spirit in 1956, Clift expressed a form of romantic maleness that was very different from the Clark Gables and Robert Taylors who had gone before. He spoke overtly of doubt, of tenderness, of alienation and uncertainty; even after illness and addiction had eaten him away, he still exposed something vulnerable in the male psyche. Thanks to this quality, and to the near manic dedication he brought to his work, Clift was a creative lodestone for two major contemporaries, Marlon Brando and James Dean, who were both scouting similar territory, and, through them, he can be seen as a spirit father both to their 'rebel' successors, like Paul Newman, Al Pacino and Johnny Depp, and even to River Phoenix and Leonardo DiCaprio, those stars who represent alternative, more feline, approaches to the complex business of being a man. 'Before you there was nothing,' John Lennon said to Elvis. Two generations of male star could offer a similar homage to Montgomery Clift.

This is a remarkable achievement by any standards, all the more so because it wasn't a long career: there were only seventeen films, although they were good enough to gain the star four Academy Award nominations. It wasn't a long life, either: thanks to booze, pills and a generally frail disposition, Clift died of heart disease just short of his forty-sixth birthday. Despite these obstacles, however, he made a living and lasting impression. For example, his early role as Matthew Garth alongside John Wayne in *Red River* is a central contribution to one of the finest Westerns ever made; as Private Robert E. Lee Prewitt in *From Here to Eternity* (1953), he set a level of subtlety and eloquence that the 1950s rarely attained. Nor did the actor need to be physically beautiful in order to make a performance sing. After the car crash, he could still grab a glorified featured role and bring home the spoils, most memorably as Perce Howland, the down-at-heel rodeo rider who teams up with Marilyn Monroe and Clark Gable in *The Misfits* (1961). In all, there is something magical about him; with one glance, one crinkle of those over-refined lips, he can take an audience captive, as well as do serious things to one impressionable boy's development.

This is the case for his importance as a screen presence. Yet does this make him that heightened Hollywood creature, a star? Brute economics suggest that it does: the Clift image is managed by the same company that pulls down the dollars for the James Dean estate, and memorabilia – photographs, magazines, deleted video titles – go for a fair price in the Amazon web auctions. In addition, although his fans in cyber space may not claim their boy is an icon first class like Jimmy, who rose and crashed with such operatic suddenness, they do sense some unique and wistful power, enough to justify the construction of well upholstered web sites.

Why the attention? No doubt the beauty has something to do with it, that rarefied, veiled, febrile beauty. Sheer loveliness, however, does not an enduring star make: if it did, Troy Donahue would be sipping nectar with the gods. As it is, there seems to be a need for some additional meaning both surrounding, and communicating itself through, the wonder-face. This book is part of a gay series, so the reader can probably guess what comes next. An essential part of Montgomery Clift's appeal lies in the fact that he loved men.

At least, part of him loved men; the jury is spending a second night in a hotel trying to work out the precise nature of his close friendships with women, with Elizabeth Taylor for example. Whatever the precise facts of the case – and so much film history is not quite history, but something less tangible, a kind of higher gossip – the actor is definitely known to have had male lovers, who drift in and out of his biographies like silent spectres from the show business closet. This silence is deepened by the fact that Clift never seems to have talked about the emotional meaning of his gay relationships, not to those friends who grant interviews to biographers at any rate; moreover, he suffers from the added burden of being a star, and witnesses, male or female, gay or straight, are apt to distort the evidence because they want to claim that their relationship alone was crucial to the great man's life. All this means that, in terms of hard facts, Clift is a near blank, a sexual and emotional enigma. Only two things can be said with any confidence: first, he adored women, and they him, and he may have slept with some of them; secondly, he slept with men and these experiences may have been at the core of his being. The rest is a matter of trying to read between the lines, which is inevitable when dealing with his particular love in his particular dark time.

The fascination with Clift, in biographies and fan material, is rooted in this darkness. He is a kind of fog, billowing to and fro across the boundaries, unclear, not only in the bedroom department, but also, much more crucially, in the question of his emotional centre. His own answer was always provisional; in fact, he never appears to have possessed himself with any confidence or clarity. The life reads like a hurricane, whirling out of control and destroying everything in its path, including, in the end, itself. Apart from the outer signs of inner turmoil – the drink, the drugs and the erratic behaviour – he had a masochistic genius for chewing himself up inside claustrophobic relationships, and his sense of identity was so uncertain that he once openly wondered whether he had swapped sexes with his twin sister in the womb. The only focus was his work, which he pursued with the stubbornness much admired by Brando and Dean. In the end, even that didn't help. His health, as well as his looks, had been destroyed by the car crash and had been worsened by his addictions; death came early, although unemployment due to insurance problems and lost friends due to his own behaviour had killed him long before. It's hard not to see the star as a tragic figure, whose chaotic life was the symptom of an emotional, sexual and spiritual confusion that ended up destroying him.

That, at least, is the conventional view, which hasn't materially changed since the first biography was published in the late 1970s. Reading these and other books, a gay writer is stricken by an unease, because Clift's star myth, if it can be called that, comes across as too general and too specific. It's too specific in its assumption that gayness and bisexuality are fixed states with fixed consequences, irrespective of individual psychology and circumstance. It's too general because it places our man outside any historical context, gay or otherwise. Overall, you get the feeling that no one is listening and hence looking: his films, in consequence, are filtered through some muzzy assumptions about sexuality and its contexts. True, stars' work is often chained to a debatable idea of who they are; nevertheless, Clift's chain seems very rusty indeed, not homophobic, but forged out of some rather quaint attitudes. This suggests that we need to give him a thorough, twenty-first century, gay going-over.

★

Montgomery Clift was born on 17 October 1920 in Omaha, Nebraska.

No. Start at the real beginning.

The Changeling's Son

For the biographers of Montgomery Clift, the real beginning was his mother, Ethel, also known as Sunny. They claim that it was she, with her smothering ways and her fantasist's monomania, who invaded his spirit, and sowed the seeds of his self-destruction. Yet, in psychological terms, the story really begins earlier with a shadowy figure called Charles Fogg, a narrow and unloving drunk who worked sporadically as a steel mill foreman in Germanstown, Pennsylvania. Charles was Sunny's adoptive father, and he made the young girl miserable. Both he and his wife told her that she was illegitimate and therefore unwanted, and the resulting search for an affirmed self lasted for the rest of Sunny's long life, and blighted her son's in turn.

The possibility of that self surfaced when the girl was eighteen. Doctor Edward E. Montgomery, who had looked after her for a year before she was farmed out for adoption, informed her that she was really the daughter of Mona Anderson, whose marriage to one Woodbury Blair had been annulled by her disapproving mother. This altered everything; it made Sunny into a changeling. For Mona had been the daughter of Colonel Robert Anderson of Virginia, the heroic Union defender of Fort Sumter during the Civil War; Woodbury's father, Montgomery Blair, had the equal prestige of having been postmaster general in Lincoln's cabinet. Thus, Ethel Fogg was an aristocrat, a 'thoroughbred' as Doctor Montgomery told her. The idea of being acknowledged by her alleged blood relatives became the obsession of her life.

This obsession didn't surface straight away, however, because there was some growing up to do. That same year, 1910, Sunny went to Cornell University where she met and fell in love with Bill Clift, an engineering student from a respectable Tennessee family. In time, they were married, and Sunny bore her husband three children. The first was Brooks, who came along in 1919; then, a year later, there were twins, Ethel (who later changed her name to Roberta) and Edward Montgomery, our star to be. By this time, Bill was doing well as first vice-president of the Omaha National Bank (engineering was never his thing). It was a good time for business, any business: these were the champagne days of the 1920s; money flowed and flappers flapped. In the specific terms of the Clift family, it meant that there was cash to spend on what became Sunny's maniacal bid to join the elite.

For, in effect, after the birth of the children, she separated from Bill, taking her offspring on extended trips to Europe that were designed, it seems, to make the junior Clifts into the princes and princesses of her imagination. It was a spangled operation of F. Scott Fitzgerald proportions. The entourage stayed at the best hotels; the children were lumbered with private tutors and a much-hated nurse called Emma Wilke; the emphasis was on crystal-cut gentility and politeness. Brooks recalled how he and his siblings weren't allowed to show anger or express opinions: 'Ma was always right.' He implies, too, that their childhood was suffocating, with the twins retreating into a self-absorbed world, where they communicated in a secret and exclusive language. The causes of his mother's behaviour are murky. The obvious reason is simply that the marriage was in trouble and that an emotionally insecure woman ran off with the children, imprisoning them in her own ice palace where she hoarded their love. The other reason is more bizarre. It involves a Blair-Anderson aunt, who inspects the children with a view to Sunny becoming accepted into the clan. This harridan, more a creature of gothic fiction than of fact, declares that the youngsters aren't up to scratch, and she keeps Sunny on a leash as the mother drags the children repeatedly round Europe in the hope of bettering them, only to be disappointed on each re-inspection. At this distance, it's impossible to get to the root of the matter, but the effects were all too clear. Rigidly controlled, cut off from other children in their glass bubble of culture, the younger Clifts had an unloving and over-controlled childhood. They were mere puppets in their mother's show, loved only for what they could be rather than for what they were.

The result, clearly, was pain; for Clift, who was the more dominated of the three, the experience was the most traumatic. Brooks remembers, a little too perfectly perhaps, how, as an adult, his brother would phone him from

Hollywood in the early hours, 'and he'd say "Boof?" – that's my childhood nickname, Boof – 'what exactly happened to us in Geneva in 1929? Was that when we caught chicken pox and learned to crochet? Did I get separated from my twin in Munich?...Were we happy then?' (He had started analysis; it shows.) 'My childhood was hobgoblin,' Clift told a journalist, 'my parents travelled a lot. That's all I can remember.' Despite this forgetfulness, though, he nursed resentments for the rest of his life; for a time, the adult star spent a period when he cut all ties with his parents. Even when diplomatic relations had been restored, communication was acrid and potentially explosive. For example, there is an account, in the days of his decline, of him rolling on the floor, exclaiming after one of his mother's more obdurate lectures, 'Oh, Ma, you are such a cunt, such a cunt!'

Why this anger existed is hard to say, but, certainly, Sunny's grip on him remained tight well beyond the usual age; if anything, it grew even tighter as he entered adolescence. The main reason was the Depression, which saw Bill unemployed for a while. Lacking the money to keep the European show on the road, the family retreated for a time to humble lodgings in Greenwich Village. (Sunny kept up appearances, though; there were silk sheets on the beds.) Then, just at the time when many boys are starting to muse about independent life, Montgomery Clift found his possibilities sealed off. Quite by chance, he became a child actor.

It happened in time-honoured fashion. In 1933, thanks to personal connections, Sunny got her son a role in a Florida stock company production of *As Husbands Go*, a fluffy drawing-room comedy. The twelve year-old was a success, and, while his sister and brother were sent away to school, he found himself making the rounds of rehearsals and auditions (he even did some modelling, which he detested). This entry into show business also meant that he acquired the inevitable child star's appendage, the stage mother. It's unclear why Sunny latched onto this role; she had been rather keen on her son entering the diplomatic service, or at least being something high class, like an artist. Still, times were hard, the Broadway theatre was culture, more or less; as time passed, her other children eventually fled her clutches by going to university, so perhaps her younger son represented a much-needed emotional bond. Whatever the case, Sunny became Mrs. Worthington, accompanying her boy everywhere. They became inseparable. Clift remained hers.

At this period, when the adolescent actor was appearing in productions like Cole Porter's *Jubilee* (staged 1935), we get the first portraits of Clift as others saw him. In his early years, he appears to have been a pretty, damped down little boy, living off Sunny's stultifying diet of culture and good breeding. His early stage period, however, reveals a more complex, and less attractive personality. The budding actor is vivacious and charming, but he is priggish, too, a stuck-up mother's boy with a dash of cruelty (he once openly taunted a pimply young colleague for being ugly). Something was happening, and it had been long delayed. This became more marked as he entered young manhood. After a break from acting during 1936 to '37, he returned to the stage and gradually began to move from anodyne roles to strong parts in worthwhile productions; in time, he moved into his own flat near his parents and began to develop his own circle of friends. It was a belated semi-independence, but it didn't have the effects that one might expect.

For, from this point on, some darker elements began to surface. Clift was charming to fellow professionals, for instance, the important ones, but he could be brusque and arrogant with lesser colleagues. He began to drink, too, and he couldn't handle it, the booze making him hysterical and violent, as if the alcohol were releasing suppressed anger or terror. At the same time, he began to develop friendships, which, observers seemed to think, contained some hidden or even sinister purpose. Some of these came out of a short-lived off-Broadway play called *Mexican Mural* (staged 1942). One of the cast members was a young actor, Kevin McCarthy, the brother of the writer Mary McCarthy, and his wife Augusta Dabney. In the following years, Clift was to become so close to the couple that there were rumours of a ménage-à -trois.

It's more likely, though, that the trio was like an off-kilter family where it's not clear who is playing what roles and where Clift, a beautiful manipulator, played hell with some loving heart strings. There were other friendships like this. For example, in the late 1930s, he had been close to a young gay conductor, Lehman Engel: after just one meeting, Clift had begun the

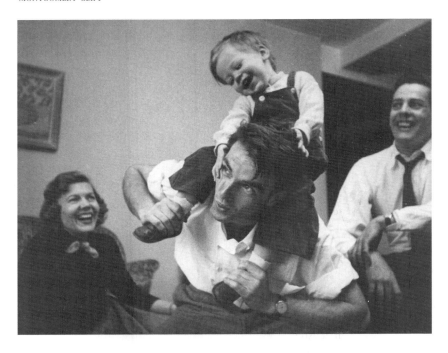

'THIS BEAUTIFUL DARLING BOY WOULD ALWAYS REMAIN A CHILD'
MONTGOMERY CLIFT WITH KEVIN McCARTHY AND FAMILY IN 1949.

friendship with a romantic gesture by seeking out Lehman at a lecture he was giving out of town. It may not have been love, but it was certainly a flirtation, and, if the relationship didn't last, then that is because so many of Clift's didn't. 'I felt our relationship couldn't be permanent,' Engel remembered later. 'I sensed that this beautiful darling boy would always remain a child. Monty was incapable of growing up.' Reading about his friends, one senses that he lunged towards people who he felt might affirm him in some way, poured a glittering light over them, and then, when the need wasn't fulfilled, snapped off the light and walked away, leaving the object of his affection confused and in the dark. Why the need wasn't fulfilled is anyone's guess, but the outcome is clear: he was a sucker for the power games that can lurk within relationships. This can be seen most vividly in his eventual closeness with two other members of the *Mexican Mural* cast, Mira Rostova and Libby Holman.

Rostova was a Russian émigré who had fled her homeland for Europe in the 1930s, and then again to the United States in 1941. She was an aspiring highbrow actress, who didn't prosper, and who gradually became Clift's acting adviser, like Paula Strasberg was to Marilyn Monroe. Once the actor's film career had begun, she was a fixture on many sets, much to the annoyance of directors, although it isn't clear what she did, apart from acting as a muse, conscience, or sounding board. Others were puzzled by this relationship, because they sensed that it involved a deep dependency on Clift's part without being romantic or overtly sexual; it was hard to read in conventional terms. The same goes for his friendship with Libby Holman, a rich, good-time girl, whom her friend, Clifton Webb, once called 'rotten ripe'. Holman had been a Broadway torch singer, had been accused of murdering her millionaire husband, had a taste for febrile gay men, and was herself believed to be lesbian. When Clift came into her orbit she wasn't in the first flush of youth, but she had the glamour of wealth and the attraction of animal energy. Yet what they meant to each other is, again, hard to determine. Some witnesses think that they had a sexual relationship; others believe that she got Clift hooked on drugs. Whatever the case, she lured him into her boozy, rackety world and held him in thrall. Both Rostova and Holman are, in fact, emblematic of the same, profound confusion between emotional love, sexual love, and the respective roles of men and women.

Certainly, Clift could choose whom he liked; he was incredibly attractive. Raised as an ersatz aristocrat, as a European as much as an American, he was also exotic, and, to add to the allure, there was something unformed about him; he was a blank canvas, which others could paint with whatever patterns they desired. This is sexy, but it implies a possible manipulation by the object of the yearning, too, an ability to wear whatever masks the adorer wishes to see. These shifting allegiances are evident in two relationships, one with a man, another with a woman, both of which occurred a little earlier, around 1940, when Clift was appearing in a big Broadway play called *There Shall Be No Night*.

The woman was Phyllis Thaxter, who had a small role as a maid. Her sophomore romance with the actor began with the two young people spending hours huddled together talking about the theatre and their ambitions, or watching old films at the Museum of Modern Art. The intensity continued after Thaxter had moved on to another show, and, at some point round this time, she has an Andy Hardy memory of Clift sliding into her bed one morning (where isn't clear), with an apparently approving Sunny serving them both breakfast. 'Monty and I loved each other very much,' Thaxter explains, 'it was a romantic kind of love – I never went to bed with him. But we finally thought – well maybe we *should* marry. It seemed like a good idea.' The idea soon failed, however. 'I've been thinking about it, darling,' Thaxter remembers him saying, 'and I can't get married. It just wouldn't be right. He seemed so serious, and a little sad, as if he knew something I didn't.' At once, she dropped the idea, sensing, she says, that 'he liked both men and women. He was absolutely wonderful to women. He felt tremendous empathy. But I also sensed he lived a very separate life when I didn't see him – a life I had no part of and never asked about.'

At about the same time as Thaxter was enjoying breakfast in bed, but not much else, an aspiring actor called 'Josh' was getting full board; he and Clift were lovers for two years. 'Our affair was for me the most beautiful experience in my life,' he gushes, 'and I'll never forget it. We were still sexually pure and rather innocent. We laughed a great deal, and played together.' Even so, there were some unnerving undercurrents. 'What floored me was Monty's ability to keep every single relationship separate and apart from every other relationship. I don't think any of his other friends knew about us, but then I didn't know any of his other friends – Monty was selfish about friendship.' Looking back over a long friendship, which carried on after the affair was over, Josh observed that '[h]e never admitted being homosexual to me, and I'd been his lover. This may sound strange, but I'm not sure he was ever exclusively homosexual, since he was capable of affectionate erotic relationships with either sex.' 'Affection' is, however, very different from 'passion'; an 'erotic relationship' is more tentative than a 'sexual', or a 'loving' one. This indicates that Clift's relationships with men and women were sealed off; their content, on any level, was vague. He could charm and mesmerise, but he was essentially a stranger, both to the loved one and to himself.

At the age of twenty, none of this matters very much: youth is, after all, the time for experiment and necessary chaos. The problem is what happens in maturity, and here Clift was vulnerable. It's possible that, if he had remained a stage actor, the hospitable bohemianism of Broadway might have helped him to hold together his loosely constructed personality. Yet life wasn't to prove so kind; Hollywood came calling. In 1946, when he was old enough to be a potential leading man, his agent, Leland Hayward, organised a six-month MGM contract so that his young client could get a subsidised taste of the film colony. This contract didn't result in work, and it ran out, but Clift did land a one-off gig for Howard Hawks, film director, producer, and a minor genius at spotting fresh talent. Hawks was about to make his epic western, *Red River*. Clift accepted the co-starring role opposite John Wayne because he hadn't worked in a while and was in debt. An ambitious man who was never sure what to be ambitious about, he stumbled into stardom. Stumbling was, in fact, the story of his career.

★

Clift hated making the film. He hated Hawks' and Wayne's macho gambolling, and he wasn't much impressed by his own work, either.

Nevertheless, his performance made an impact, and for unusual reasons. *Red River* had been shot in 1946, but, thanks to distribution and legal problems, it wasn't released until 1948, within a few weeks of *The Search*, Clift's second film, a more arty effort directed by Fred Zinnemann. Thus, in true show business fashion, the critics and public got a double dose of the actor in the roles of a heroic cowboy and a sensitive G.I., the kind of contrast that grabs headlines and suggests unusual gifts. Taken together, these two roles, along with an Academy Award nomination for *The Search*, confirmed Clift as the new, big thing. At once, the nonsense began, the rounds of interviews and the magazine covers, the intrusion of fans idling outside his New York flat, the end of privacy. For the first few years, however, nothing could stop his ascent. Although he preferred to remain a freelance, not a player on a long-term contract to any particular studio, Clift did sign a three picture deal with Paramount in the late 1940s, the second film of which, *A Place in the Sun*, brought him together for the first time with Elizabeth Taylor.

This relationship has fascinated biographers of both stars, partly because its sexual component is unclear, and partly because the physical beauty of the couple creates an imaginative need: as two gorgeous surfaces, they sing together; the image speaks of the eternal romantic high. Still, appearance isn't always meaning; what Clift and Taylor meant to each other can't be reduced to a simple matter of sex.

It all began simply enough. The story goes that the duo first met in 1949, at the premiere of *The Heiress*, which was released that year as Clift's first project under the three-picture deal. The occasion was a standard publicity stunt: both stars were to start shooting *A Place in the Sun* for Paramount, and therefore the celebrity heat was on. It's no wonder, then, that this first meeting was surrounded by heightened emotion and anxiety. For instance, Clift wasn't in the best of states that night; he had a hangover. He hated these junkets, too, and had tried to get out of the commitment by claiming that he didn't have a tuxedo. Worse, once he and Taylor had made their royal progress into the auditorium, there was the agony of watching his performance. All told, the evening sounds like a nightmare; under these conditions, it's almost unavoidable that enemies (the studio, Hollywood itself, even one's own glittering image) are conjured up out of nowhere, and that, conversely, allies and sympathetic spirits are sought out.

It doesn't take much imagination to see that Taylor was likely to be one of these spirits. She was seventeen years old at the time, a former child star, who had been loaned out by MGM for her first fully adult role. Yet she was more than a tongue-tied ingénue; the word 'feisty' could have been coined for her. Although she was Clift's junior by eleven years, she was far more experienced in the Hollywood game; where he was a kind of walking mist, she was, on the surface at least, as direct as a slap across the face. There were significant similarities, too. Taylor shared Clift's wit and native intelligence; she, like him, had a domineering mother; her emotions were as volatile as his; above all, her early years had been spent in England; like her glamorous partner, she had been partly formed by an older culture. In other words, here was Clift's spiritual complement. It's no surprise that, intimidated by the premiere and its ballyhoo, they latched on to one another.

The sign of the affinity was a nickname. As the character of Morris Townsend wandered across the screen, Clift, who was sitting next to Taylor, offered a running commentary on his performance: 'I'm so awful, Bessie Mae, I'm so awful!'... 'Let's get out of here, Bessie Mae.' '...[t]he whole world knows you as Elizabeth Taylor; only I can call you Bessie Mae.' It's impossible to say whether these statements were ever made, but the nickname did exist. One Taylor biographer, Donald Spoto, believes it to be an elision of her shortened first name and *Besame mucho*, a popular Latin American song of the period. Whatever the case, the crucial point is that Clift gave her a moniker, as he did to all his intimates (for instance, Ned Smith, a friend from the earliest days, was known as 'Smythe'). This is psychologically important, because a nickname is a form of conspiracy; it binds together the namer and the named in apparent intimacy, while the playfulness suggests that there are definite, if unspecified, limits. In fact, that is all one can say about this couple; fluidity reigned. Their story basically amounts to Taylor and Clift did/didn't/could have slept together, and they did/didn't/might have contemplated marriage (delete according to personal inclination). Once again, Montgomery Clift eludes us: he could offer the loved one the illusion of closeness, but the

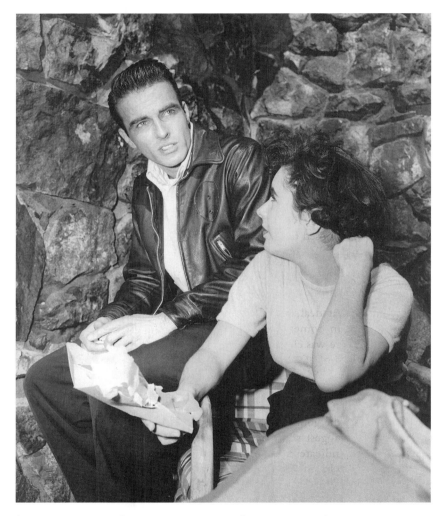

'SOME OF THE MEN I'VE REALLY LIKED DIDN'T LIKE WOMEN.'
MONTGOMERY CLIFT AND ELISABETH TAYLOR ON THE SET OF
A PLACE IN THE SUN IN 1949.

intensity could waver like an inadequate electric current. He comes across as a disappointing man.

To begin with, though, once the premiere was behind them and the two stars had stepped before the cameras for *A Place in the Sun*, intensity was the dominant note. George Stevens was a demanding director, and, in consequence, Clift seems to have been both a mentor to Taylor, encouraging, guiding, rehearsing with her in private, and a schoolgirl chum, helping her through the inevitable discomforts of film making, especially on location. This experience was overwhelming for the young actress: Clift offered her a new, more serious vision of her craft; the attention and concentration on her as a woman was affirming and awakening. It's clear that she entertained hopes, as a Victorian novelist might have said, but her recorded comments over the years suggest that hers were very different from Clift's. During the shoot, for example, he is supposed to have exclaimed to her, 'I've found my other half!' Later, he told an Italian gossip columnist that she was 'my ideal woman,' his 'twin': '[w]e are so much alike it's *fantastic*!' By contrast, after Clift's death, Taylor told Truman Capote, 'one doesn't always fry the fish one wants to fry. Some of the men I've really liked didn't like women.' These fragments don't amount to a great deal, especially as they are reports of reports, and the Capote quotation comes from Kitty Kelley, who is no Claire Tomalin. Nevertheless, there was clearly closeness, tenderness and deep feeling: after the initial excitement of 1949, both remained strong friends, although Taylor's booming stardom and ongoing marital soap opera, and Clift's decline and addictions, created difficulties and silences. In addition, sexual feeling was probably present for Taylor at some point, and, for all we know, Clift was happy to deliver the goods. Still, his words – 'ideal woman', 'twin', 'we are so much alike' – suggest something greater and lesser than a simply sexual outlook. They indicate the desire for a feminine shadow, an equivalent, perhaps, of the twin sister with whom he shared a childhood secret language. We don't know enough about this sister, or the relationship, to be sure of this. All the same, the shadow woman is a consistent theme in Clift's life. With Taylor, as with others, it began as a private communion as he and the chosen woman mutually searched for each other through a specific acting task. Mira Rostova is an example, as is Phyllis Thaxter, and, in 1953, Donna Reed in

From Here to Eternity. In Reed's case, filming was as far as the matter went. Yet other cases, like that of Myrna Loy in the later 1950s, became yearning friendships, which didn't and couldn't last, because the needs of both people were out of kilter. This is the keynote of the Taylor–Clift relationship: it was a love story with an ellipsis at its heart. For a man like Clift, the strain, and the feeling of not reaching the desired destination, must have been severe.

Nor was the career any substitute for his lack of personal definition; if anything, it made matters worse by piling on expectations that he wasn't equipped to fulfil. Although *A Place in the Sun* confirmed his power as a new, edgier kind of star (Stevens spent ages over the editing; it wasn't released until 1951), the ethos of Hollywood appalled him, and so the 1950s began to mark the desperate use of alcohol, of uppers, downers, and maybe harder substances, to keep himself together. It wasn't until the filming of *From Here to Eternity* in 1953, however, that he began to booze openly on set, so openly that, according to one biographer, his role in Frank Sinatra's famous death scene had to be cut down because he was too sozzled to finish it. It was round this time, too, that old friendships cooled, thanks to his behaviour (susceptible to blackouts, he nearly dropped the McCarthy's baby; they never invited him to their house again), or because, self-destructively, he was happy to break the ties himself. (On *From Here to Eternity*, for example, he was prepared to do without Rostova.) As a result, his roots weakened.

None of this helped his career. He had already made some strange decisions; for example, he had pulled out of his third Paramount film, *Sunset Boulevard* (1950), because he had been unhappy with the role. (It went to William Holden, and it marked the last time Clift ever had a deal with a studio for more than one film). Also, biographies, and his own later interviews, suggest that during this decade he was offered a number of desirable roles, although one must be careful with the specifics; claims that he rejected the James Dean role in *East of Eden* (1955), for instance, may be just a retrospective angling for prestige. One thing is certain, however. Now, in his mid-thirties, after Oscar nominations for *The Search*, *A Place in the Sun* and *From Here to Eternity*, at a time when one might have expected him to push his career forward, he vacillated, as if his creative engine had stalled.

From the spring of 1953 to the spring of 1956, three vital years for a leading man of his age, he did no work at all, apart from a disappointing staging of Chekhov's *The Seagull*. Robert LaGuardia, his first biographer, presents an image of futility, of a man fiddling around with scripts and other material sent by his agency: 'Monty typed up meticulous lists of everything he received, dividing the tally into books, plays, and movie scripts: he would then log in the date the item was received, who the producer or director was, the terms of the offer, and later log in when the item was returned – all in separate, neat columns. Nothing he read interested him; but he loved going through the elaborate sorting process.' If this is true (LaGuardia doesn't give a source), it suggests a serious psychological freezing.

Thanks to this dithering and chaos, these were fatally misspent years. Instead of consolidating his career, Clift cavorted with Libby Holman, held louche dinner parties, saw a psychiatrist, gay himself, who friends believed did nothing but encourage the star's excesses, and frittered away what was left of his youth while Marlon Brando and James Dean began to lay claim to his crown. Only when money was pressing, and the possibility arose of working again with his beloved Bessie Mae, did he crawl out of the mire and accept the lead in *Raintree County* (1957), a big budget MGM soap opera set during the American Civil War. He wasn't in a fit state to take on this job. Indeed, the only reason he kept going was a bag, which contained booze and heaven alone knows what else. Thus, unfocused and fragile, he staggered towards 12 May 1956 and the disaster of his life.

★

It's unclear why Clift wrapped his car round a telephone pole on that evening. He had been attending a low-key party at Elizabeth Taylor's Los Angeles house, but everyone present – accounts vary, but the main candidates are Taylor's husband Michael Wilding, Kevin McCarthy and Rock Hudson and his future wife, Phyllis Gates – said that he had only drunk a couple of glasses of wine; again, there have been disagreements. Still, whatever was or wasn't sloshing around inside him, he had left the gathering quite early, at the same time as McCarthy, and had followed his friend's car down one of the many winding roads in Coldwater Canyon. After a while, his friend noticed through his rear view mirror that the star's own vehicle seemed to be edging dangerously close; later, he saw it swerving erratically. Then, McCarthy says, he heard a crash and saw a cloud of dust. Alarmed, he drove back and found a mangled wreck with Clift curled under the dashboard, his face a bloody pulp. Fearing that his friend was dead, McCarthy rushed back to Taylor's house for help. When the rest of the party returned to the scene, it became clear that Clift was alive, but seriously injured. A horrified Taylor, covering herself in blood, cradled him in her arms, and accompanied him to the hospital, where it was discovered that his nose was broken, his jaw crushed, and that the left side of his face had been heavily lacerated. He was in terrible pain: the jaw had to be wired and he was suffering from severe whiplash.

The star spent nine weeks recovering, while back at MGM, executives put the production on hold. Aware of his reputation, they had wisely taken out insurance, so the star would have been well within his rights to abandon the project and look after himself. All the same, he struggled back to work, sensing, perhaps, that if he didn't, he might be labelled as an addict who couldn't finish a job. Certainly he took the hardest course. Camera personnel had to concentrate on the side of his face that wasn't stiff and wired up; painkillers and drink, along with barbiturates and tranquilisers, numbed him. He finished the film, but the damage had been done, not only to his looks, but also to his sense of self-definition.

This was demonstrated one Saturday, while he was resting after the shoot was over; a friend and fellow actor, Jack Larson, came to visit him at what sounds like a rented Los Angeles house. After the two men had spent some time lounging round the pool, Clift disappeared inside, and he didn't come out for half an hour. Puzzled, Larson entered the house in order to find out where he was. On reaching the kitchen, he heard a moaning sound; he called, but there was no answer. Then he entered the bedroom, and saw the curtains torn down, and the room filled with Californian sunlight. There was Clift, sitting in a corner, sobbing. Larson crept back to the pool. Much later, the star approached him and touched his arm. His friend recalls what he said and how he said it: "'Jack... when I went into the bedroom I looked at myself in the mirror. Really looked at myself for the first time," and he began to choke up. "You know what?" His eyes filled with tears. "I think I can still act. I think I still have a career.'" This was both true and untrue. For the remainder of the 1950s, Clift got work; he made about a film a year. Nevertheless, he was no longer a star of the first rank. With or without the accident, he was pushing forty, and, consciously or unconsciously, he had abandoned his place in the sun. As a result, his remaining nine years were lived in the shade of a disconnected despair.

Anecdotes confirming this are sprinkled throughout the last pages of his biographies; they give the impression of a life careering out of control. For instance, in Rome, filming *The Young Lions* (1958), the first work he did after the crash, the damaged star vanished, only to be found later in a seedy brothel. On another occasion on the same shoot, he leapt on top of a car, and performed a manic dance until he collapsed. In fact, from now on, every Clift set was a battleground on which the forces of self-destruction clashed with a fervent desire to communicate what remained of his gift on celluloid. Sometimes, it was a close run thing: *Lonelyhearts* (1959) required short days and cue cards.

A similar struggle took place in his relationships during this period; many people drifted away, or loosened their connection. Yet, just because the biographers have dug up stories of cruising, Dionysian rites in a Christopher Street bar, of sailors and hustlers wandering in and out of his New York brownstone, this doesn't justify their suggestion that Clift had simply plunged into a morass of seediness and promiscuity. On the contrary, this later period contains two opposing tendencies. The first is the kind of excess just described; the second is the countervailing attempt to settle down, to normalise himself.

In short, he tried marriage. Sometime around the filming of *The Young Lions*, he met a pseudonymous Frenchman called 'Giles'. This young man, who had ambitions in the fashion industry, eventually abandoned them around 1958 to become Clift's partner, kept man, unofficial pimp, or drug dealer, depending on what witness one cares to believe. The details of this story are lost; Giles himself never gave his version. In consequence, the testimony of outsiders has turned the relationship into a version of *The Servant* (1963), in which Giles is the parasite and pander, and the star a passive dupe of his partner's wicked, queeny ways. This is too neat to be true, but there is no doubt that they were a turbulent and destructive couple, although the more accurate film analogy would be *Who's Afraid of Virginia Woolf?* (1966), with Clift and Giles as Richard Burton and Elizabeth Taylor fighting and verbally tearing each other to shreds, while the dinner guests blink over the wine goblets. In time, concerned friends eased Giles out. Another door closed.

Yet it would be a mistake to see the Clift of the late 1950s as a doped-up Eeyore, glumly surveying the dandelions; as so often, his compartmentalised world obscures other sides of his nature. For example, in 1959, he came to Britain to make the film version of Tennessee Williams' *Suddenly, Last Summer* at Shepperton Studios, just outside London: it featured Katherine Hepburn and Taylor; this was Bessie Mae's third teaming with her old friend. During the production, Clift stayed at a sleek London hotel, and here he came across Maurice Leonard, a future television producer and biographer of the star, but, back then, a humble switchboard operator. Between shifts (and sometimes during them), the boy and the man had a fling. Despite Clift's manic intensity, his screaming night terrors, and what might be called a puppyish desperation, Leonard's most dominant memories are of tenderness, generosity, and fun: 'I never saw him depressed – worried occasionally and sometimes annoyed – but not depressed. I learnt later that he was anxious about his career during that time, but he certainly kept it from me. We laughed a lot while he was making *Suddenly, Last Summer.*' This is as partial a viewpoint as anyone else's, and Leonard was very young. Nevertheless, it suggests a richer portrait of Clift than the usual, one-dimensional picture of the film star sliding into hell. Any man who can do an Edith Evans impersonation can claim to have an innate buoyancy, if nothing else.

Suddenly, Last Summer isn't a good film. By then, in fact, Clift's career was a thing of shreds and patches, and the nadir came in 1961 when the director John Huston, who had worked amicably with him on *The Misfits* that year, offered the lead role in *Freud* (1962), a highbrow biopic whose original script had been written by Jean-Paul Sartre. Yet this promising combination of subject and personnel didn't result in a good film, or a happy experience. If, up to this point, Clift had been living an epilogue, then this production rang down the curtain.

As so often with Hollywood history, the truth of what happened depends on whose gossip gets the most credence. For his part, Huston believed that he was betrayed: an actor he admired and trusted turned out to be a shambling wreck who held up production because he had trouble learning his lines. Clift's supporters, on the other hand, claim that Huston himself was the problem. An action man baffled by an interior theme, a director forced to rewrite Sartre's unworkable screenplay during the shoot itself, he was a bully venting his frustrations on the nearest available victim, and this turned out to be his star. In addition, it's possible that Huston had caught Clift in bed with another man, and this shock, his detractors suggest, awoke insecurities in the cigar-chewing, macho film-maker. Certainly, Huston gave Clift the directorial works: he yelled, insisted on long takes when it was clear that the actor couldn't sustain them, came up with rewritten dialogue at the last minute, and split the company into two distinct camps. With a budget out of control and a cast in rebellion, Huston managed to finish the film, but someone had to pay for the delays. Clift was that someone. There were suits concerning overspend and the deliberate refusal to learn lines; there were countersuits concerning the star's outstanding fee, the whole weary rigmarole of post-production vindictiveness. In the end, he got his money, but he walked away from the wreckage bearing stardom's equivalent of leprosy. The industry now deemed him to be uninsurable.

Without work, therefore, he entered his final phase, one in which he didn't care about himself or his reputation. Hustlers, pick-ups, the occasional drug dealer, wandered through his life; also, ill-health took hold (he had never been strong in the first place; for instance, the ongoing effects of an attack of amoebic dysentery in 1939 had kept him out of the army). He had developed cataracts; he had a calcium deficiency and varicose veins; he was knocking back painkillers and other pills just for the hell of it. With a new minder, Lorenzo James, he tottered, like King Lear, across the blasted heath of Manhattan.

Things brightened when Elizabeth Taylor offered to put up her leading lady's fee in lieu of insurance so that he could star alongside her in an adaptation of Carson McCuller's novel, *Reflections in a Golden Eye* (1941), an overheated tale of frustration and desire on a Southern army base; he would have played her husband, a closet gay officer. (The director, by the way, was to be John Huston. Everyone must have been desperate, or optimistic.) Yet Clift was fated never to play a gay character (after his death, the job went to Marlon Brando), because he first went to Germany to film *The Defector* (1966), a dreary Cold War thriller, which he may have undertaken to show that he had the staying power for the more important film. It was a strenuous shoot; frail and prematurely old as he was, he undertook all the action scenes himself, and the strain was too much. On 23 July 1966, Lorenzo James went to his bedroom to wake him and found him stretched out on his bed, dead from a heart attack. He was only in his mid-forties. As might be expected, the obituaries praised his gifts and lamented his failure to fulfil them. In later interviews and reminiscences, the people who had known him remembered his charm, beauty and self-destructiveness. It was another failed life. The history of stardom is full of them. Failure is, in fact, part of the wonder of it all, the human element that binds the glory on the screen to the small, compromised lives of its spectators. In this respect, Montgomery Clift had fulfilled his promise. Like Marilyn Monroe, or James Dean, he had been a remarkable rocket, which had stopped short in mid-trajectory, leaving behind nothing but questions. It was left to others' imaginations to create a coherent meaning out of the wreckage.

Those others are the biographers and, through them, the fans. Both create a connection between their judgement on the man and their response to the films, calling up the tired old paradox whereby someone who can't hack it in everyday life is granted magical gifts and privileged perceptions on the creative plane. These are defined as heightened emotional qualities, both too deep and too vulnerable, and they are identified by specific words such as 'intensity', 'angst', 'fragility', or (a favourite) 'ambiguity'. The Movie Actors web page most succinctly captures this life-art connection when it states that Clift's portrayal of Perce Howland in *The Misfits* is 'one of the great ones of his career – a man with physical and mental scars… Perhaps it was so good because there was so much of himself in the character.' There is a kind of equation here: deep suffering equals magic powers equals a special presence flickering across Row H. The being of existence and the seeming of the screen are locked in a complex dance. It's a standard response, the Clift myth, in fact.

The question is whether it's the right response: if you misinterpret the life then you may misinterpret the work, or get the two muddled up. This is especially difficult when the star is gay, or, in Clift's case, has a gay element in his make-up, because a personal judgement about what gayness is or does can be a reflection more of the writer's preconceptions than of the actual case. The time has now come to tackle these problems. First, we need to go back to the beginning, not of his life, but of his stardom. For stars are born in a tight wrapping of words, and this wrapping, tied by others, can imprison them.

The Vanishing Man

About a decade after Clift's death, two detailed biographies turned up in quick succession, like long-delayed buses. The first has been met in passing. This was Robert LaGuardia's *Monty: A Biography of Montgomery Clift* in 1977; the second, Patricia Bosworth's *Montgomery Clift: A Biography*, reached the bookshops a year later. Of the two, LaGuardia was the more melodramatic and Bosworth the more subtle: she had extra material on the childhood, too, having unearthed the Anderson-Blair connection. Nevertheless, the two books are very similar in their outlook, technique and persuasiveness, so much so that they set the terms and conditions for two later writers, Barney Hoskyns (*Montgomery Clift: Beautiful Loser*, 1991) and Maurice Leonard, the obliging switchboard operator (*Montgomery Clift*, 1997), who both follow the same contours and who work within the same assumptions. Challenge LaGuardia and Bosworth, therefore, and you chip away at the very edifice of the Clift myth.

The keystone of that edifice is the idea of spiritual indeterminacy, a fundamental inability to be a male, which, according to the biographers, creates the personal and professional failure, the destruction and the addiction. All of this is rooted in a sexual limbo defined as 'bisexuality', which eventually turns into 'exclusive homosexuality' during the Giles period, and which can be traced back to Sunny, the woman who disrupted her son's male integrity and doomed him to a provisional existence whose inevitable outcome was psychic breakdown. For them, the story is about the tragedy of doubleness; they admire and sympathise with their subject because they believe that, to quote R.E.M, 'Monty got a raw deal'. Put like that, it seems a straightforward and sympathetic approach. Yet, reading these biographies and their successors, you are struck by a sense of staleness and limit, of something not fully acknowledged. There is one brutal reason for this: these writers are journalists, good ones, but they rely on newspaper cuttings and eyewitness accounts, which, by their nature, are soaked in the outlook of a specific time. Therefore, no matter how eager LaGuardia, Bosworth and company may be to discover their subject's inner voice, they end up reproducing someone else's. These judgements are crucial, and they need unpicking.

It's all a matter of context, and that context is the America, and film star journalism, of the immediate post-war period. The 1950s in particular were a grim time for gay people; a number of writers have noted how that low, dishonest decade was nervous about any way of living, or seeming, that questioned marriage, male dominance and the world according to *Ozzie and Harriet*. One of the reasons was the Cold War. Faced with forces that could undermine everything that capitalism held dear, the authorities laid down some paradoxically restrictive rules about the nature of all-American freedom. Another reason was rooted in the war that had just been won. For the exodus of young men into the armed services had fractured family structures, already weakened by the Depression, and some had enjoyed gay experiences that otherwise might not have happened. Part of the post-war reconstruction, in consequence, was an attempt to push gender and sexuality back into their orthodox boxes so that everyone could knuckle down and contribute to the forthcoming consumer boom.

Hollywood had enjoyed a boom itself during the war, so it had no reason to rock this particular boat. Its films, in fact, and above all its publicity apparatus, played a complex role in the project. What is not complex are the fan books. Looking at them today, with their plastic smiles and sleek interiors, one senses that the moneyed glamour is a veiled come-on to the public: you, too, can get these goodies, if you conform to the established roles. The most important role was, clearly, heterosexuality, but, in terms of Hollywood men, this wasn't enough: male stars had to be seen to be male by pairing themselves publicly with a suitable female. When this didn't happen, when Anthony Perkins, for instance, appeared to be getting too chummy with Tab Hunter, studio bosses were quick to hitch both actors to an unattached starlet for the benefit of the cameras. Being a bachelor star was all right, it seemed, but being a lone bachelor star, wandering like an outlaw outside the accepted structure, was a little disturbing.

Early on in his career, thanks in part to his public scepticism about Hollywood and its mores (privately, he had called it 'Vomit, California'; his press interviews were more polite, but just as critical), Clift acquired these huckleberry qualities, and he never quite threw them off. Much of the journalism in papers and fan magazines is an attempt to place him within the standard guy and gal language. As a gal didn't exist, a kind of linguistic polyfilla was concocted to cover the cracks. To begin with, writers followed the standard procedure of linking Clift to any passing minor actress, but, as time passed, these imaginary wild oats seemed to go on for too long and frustration began to creep in. (His failure to get it together with Elizabeth Taylor must have been a major disappointment.). Thus, there were headlines like 'Monty's Odd Secret', 'Montgomery Clift: His Stranger Than Fiction Romance', and (this is a killer) 'Are Girls Too Swift for Montgomery Clift?' In 1954, *Modern Screen* built a whole thesis round 'What Makes Monty Run?', claiming that 'it isn't arrogance that makes Clift hide from the public, flee from romance. It's a deep-rooted fear of failure that's turned him into filmdom's Vanishing Man.' On one level, the journalists had nothing to report, so they worked within the great tradition of making things up. At a deeper level, though, they were expressing a profound unease. Their words suggest this: 'odd', 'stranger', 'vanishing', 'flee', all indicate non-being and instability. Whatever they knew or didn't know about the star's private life, it's clear that they were exercised by the fact that he didn't fit into public or social standards as they perceived them. For this reason, they created an image of creepy mystery. You sense that they were unsettled by some fundamental failure in what might be called Clift's male gesture.

The biographers, who were equally hamstrung by the difficulties surrounding his silence about his emotional life, inherited this outlook and emphasis. Their books, in consequence, are little more than a sophisticated version of the 1950s headlines, augmented by the observations of friends who work within the same pattern of feeling. It's a muddled pattern, which manages to combine sympathy for the struggles of men like Clift, anxiety about their becoming close to women, along with a nail-biting concern about unorthodox sexuality engendering disease and collapse. In their hands, the star becomes a generalised example of bisexuality as a disruption of maleness, which corrupts the accepted divisions between him and her, masculinity and femininity.

These attitudes can be seen very early on in the rhetorical devices they apply to Sunny. Their whole interpretation springs from their assumption of what the third biographer, Barney Hoskyns, neatly sums up as 'Oedipal (s)mothering'. LaGuardia was the first to establish the idea that mother domination was a key to the story. Writing on Clift's adolescence, for example, he notes that 'the boy still had to deal with his mother's smothering ways', then he collapses into a flurry of imponderable questions: 'What was it with Monty? He was obviously strong-willed.... He was annoyed by her oppressive presence, yet never once did he ever show a sign of rebellion towards her – strange, in view of the fact that Monty was not a submissive boy. What is even stranger is that Monty was at an age when most children go through a kind of identity crisis, in which they often pout and complain about always being told what to do. Why wasn't Monty going through the same kind of overt adolescent rebellion? His obviously repressed resentment would bear violent fruit later on.' Elsewhere, he quotes the actor's friend, Ned Smith, who said that Clift had a great impact on his life, but 'I'm never sure whether the influence on me was from his mother on him, because his mother told him what to do. He was never able to be a person on his own, and when he tried, he lost.' LaGuardia presses home this idea of a psychic manacle when he gets to the erratic behaviour of Clift's early manhood. He reduces this to 'an eerie version of Monty's childhood. That child had contained cracks, poor buttressing, incompletions – and, like a house falling in on its poorly constructed basement, Monty, under the mounting pressures of independent adulthood, and the attempt to acquire a new *person*, was caving in on himself. Before, there had always been Ethel to keep the house from falling. Ironically, and perhaps unwittingly, she had arranged the design of her support so that any ultimate rejection after would force the house to crumble.'

LaGuardia doesn't quite say that mommie dearest makes you queer, but queerishness, as an element in Clift's fluidity, clearly troubles him. As his diction suggests – 'repressed resentment', 'violent fruit', and all of that Fall of the House of Clift passage – he is more concerned with an idea of male collapse, the suggestion being that Sunny launched a sustained attack on her son's very God-given manhood, occupied him like an alien army, and ate away at his health and spiritual integrity. Bosworth works more delicately within this same pattern, using her discovery of the Anderson-Blair connection to create a fresh psychological motive for the same female intrusion and distortion of manly rightness.

In this context, gayness is a mere element of the wider problem, and it gets short shrift. Both biographers chose to underplay or ignore questions about Clift's gay life or context. For example, both interview a couple of lovers, but these witnesses are presented as hermetically sealed sound bites. We have met 'Josh' already; LaGuardia offers 'Rick', another lover (presumably) from the Broadway days, who is invited back to the actor's flat. To keep the testimony within the bounds of his own perceptions, the biographer gets an editorial in first. 'The scene which ensued,' he declares, 'had it been between a man and a woman in a first-draft movie script, might have been presented as Romantic Cliché Number Sixty-two.' "I was about to leave", says Rick, "when Monty helped me on with my raincoat. He was behind me; I felt his hand touching me while he helped me on with the raincoat. Some blip must have happened, and we both knew that we wanted each other. He kissed me, and then said, surprised, something like, "I had no idea..." Well, I had no idea about him either. We went to bed.' This appears to have been the beginning of a relationship, but, in the following pages, LaGuardia does very little to present it as such. His writing isolates the two men in a room. What 'Rick' and Clift thought about the experience isn't considered, nor is there any testimony from 'Giles'. In all, gay being is reduced to a lonely fumble in a bed. It's something that you suffer from, like bed wetting, as Christopher Isherwood once put it.

The writers also imply that, like an embarrassing nocturnal accident, the problem has certain effects, but they don't go very far in defining them. LaGuardia offers Arthur Miller saying that Clift 'was struggling with his homosexuality. He lived in a period, unfortunately, when these things were unacceptable in any disguise... This struggle that he secretly fought caused him great guilt', while Bosworth quotes the screenwriter Arthur Laurents: 'Monty was miserable. He was totally guilt-ridden about his homosexuality.' Gayness, makes you guilty, then, but it doesn't have any meaning beyond that.

In fairness, a lack of articulate testimony might well have limited the writers' room for manoeuvre. They get into far deeper difficulties, however, when they are faced with Clift and women, where there is no shortage of evidence. All would be well, one suspects, if he could be seen as an uncomplicated gay star who went round with women as a cover up. Unfortunately, there was closeness in Clift's female friendships, there may even have been love, but because nothing is completely clear, the writers have to work hard to give meaning to male and female relationships where the orthodox sexual dance doesn't seem to have gone on. LaGuardia, in particular, takes refuge in ungainly psychology. Writing about the early days with Taylor, he notes that 'Monty seemed to have a need to "confess" to young women, as if somehow, in burdening them with his sexual conflicts, he could release himself from his inhibitions and be free to love honestly.' The underlying attitude here is the same in both writers. For them, a man must be linked to a woman by physical desire, even if he is only 'confessing' to an urge that doesn't include her. The richness of intimacy is sacrificed to conventional expectations of how a man should carry on with the opposite sex.

Because he doesn't do this, he must be a broken creature. Bosworth quotes Mira Rostova's view that the star was 'totally split sexually... That was the core of his tragedy, because he never stopped being conflicted and he never stopped feeling guilty about being conflicted'. The biographer adds a gloss. 'It was this conflict,' she asserts, without any evidence whatsoever '– this warring between his yielding receptive feminine side and his self-asserting questing side – that prevented him from ever realizing complete fulfilment'; the tension, she claims, made him unable to love anyone fully. It follows from this line of feeling that any alternative way of being is strange, or wrong, and must involve some psychic disturbance.

At this point, the biographers are on safer ground, because it's indisputable that Clift was as disturbed as they come. To help matters, the precise evidence of his addictions is foggy, so their meaning is open to any interpretation one cares to apply. In LaGuardia and Bosworth's case, they take very different substances – alcohol, uppers, downers and pills taken for separate medical reasons – and pour them into one undifferentiated can labelled 'violent fruit'. The aim is metaphorical: it's an extension of LaGuardia's collapsing house in which Clift's structure is so inherently unstable that it's bound to fall in on itself.

This sense of moral inevitability is most cunningly implied in Bosworth's book; in fact, it's her major contribution to the rhetoric. She frames her story with a prologue about the crash, which takes us, step by step, through the events surrounding Elizabeth Taylor's party and presents Kevin McCarthy's testimony about the fateful drive home. Then her pitch rises as she describes Taylor scrambling over the front seat and cradling Clift's head in her lap: 'She looked down into his face, which was a bloody unrecognisable pulp. He stirred in her arms and moaned. He was alive, but his nose was broken, his jaw shattered, his cheeks severely lacerated, and his upper lip split completely in half.' Clift's looks, then, have been destroyed, but he isn't James Dean; he has survived his particular accident. With one wave of the wand, however, Bosworth bumps him off: 'Montgomery Clift survived that night and lived for ten more years, but his real death occurred as he lay bleeding and half-conscious in Elizabeth Taylor's arms. Nothing would ever be the same for him after that.' The 'real death' idea is important. From the very outset, it encourages the reader to think that Clift was fated to suffer a special punishment, a death in life, as if he were a Dorian Gray who had turned into his portrait but had spookily survived. Bosworth's prologue, in effect, fixes our perceptions. It suggests that this story is going to be about the inevitable consequences of sexual transgression. On the whole, the Clift myth is about paying a price for difference. The biographers don't put it like that, but their narrative pattern leads to that conclusion. For them, there is an inherent threat in the star's way of living and being, but this exists only because of their interpretation of three particular words. Change these readings, and Clift himself changes.

The first word is 'normality'; the writers never openly use it, but one can imagine their lips moving as they interview witnesses and hammer on their typewriters. They work on the premise, first, that it's a fixed essence, and therefore a reliable yardstick for measuring the nature of Clift's being, and, secondly, that it's defined by the sexual act alone. This act can be heterosexual (good), or homosexual (bad), the suggestion being that we are born into a world where these meanings have all been worked out in advance and are therefore timeless and immutable. Logically, then, if you are made in a different way, there must be something wrong with you. That something is, implicitly, the second word, 'bisexuality'. Over the years, there have been numerous readings of this term, but the biographers are consistent in their own response. They see it as a non-state, neither one thing nor the other: in their eyes, it engenders chaos; it's a form of betrayal, in which the fixed positions of men and women, masculinity and femininity, are elided and thereby dangerously weakened. The language of the Fifties journalists hints at this feeling, but the book writers, with their greater space and resources, make it clear, although they aren't fully conscious of doing so.

'Bisexuality' is a convenient label for the maelstrom of urges and needs running throughout Clift's story, but it doesn't do much to capture specific states and experiences. It's mildly unhelpful, in fact, and, since the star's day, sociologists and theorists of identity politics have tried to get to its meaning, if it has any, in a number of different ways and from a variety of perspectives. One of the most useful of these approaches takes as its starting point the human need for intimacy; gender and sexuality are secondary considerations. According to this approach, suggested in Fred Klein's *The Bisexual Option: A Concept of One Hundred Per Cent Intimacy* (1978), men and women desire, above all, emotional closeness. Sex is the ultimate expression of this. In fact, he argues, promiscuity can be seen as an attempt to achieve intimacy by desperately pursuing its outward form, as if you could evoke love simply by blowing a kiss. Yet, the theory implies, the person you are intimate with isn't fixed only to the opposite sex.

From this, it can be deduced that we go to others, men or women, with different needs at different times, sometimes during the course of the same day, sometimes even the same hour. In this respect, the walls dividing heterosexuality from homosexuality, or bisexuality from both, are porous. Rostova's idea of the split assumes fixed states, whereas they are no such thing.

On the contrary (so the theory suggests), a relationship can be emotionally intimate without any sexual energy; it can be sensual, although sex merely hovers vaguely in the air; it can be erotic, that is, have a sexual tingle that both parties acknowledge but choose not to pursue, or it can be the full blown thing. To complicate, and enrich, matters further, it can be all of these things, depending on the situation and the nature of the people involved. It follows that the language used to define our emotional or sexual nature – 'gay', 'straight', 'bisexual' – are, at best, blanket terms, which don't help to make clear what can be very fluid and paradoxical states.

The realities are further blurred by subsidiary terms, like 'masculine' and 'feminine', which trail behind the sexual definitions and exacerbate the problem. Bosworth's gloss on Clift's 'yielding receptive feminine side and his self-asserting questing side' operates within this context. The Clift biographers work within the questionable intellectual convention that believes what you do in bed is the major element in deciding who you are. It contains the confused idea that gay, or gayish, men are substitute women, who possess specific qualities, like femininity, by virtue of their same sex attraction. This muddle is a judgement on individual feeling and desire that perhaps only the individual could answer.

Certainly, some of the ideas we have seen – the collapse, the gender storm, the inevitable doom – might not be the terms in which Clift would have framed his experience; their language is imposed on him. Yet here is the ultimate conundrum about his self-definition: how can I, Edward Montgomery Clift, define my needs, yearnings and emotions if the dominant language, whether that means words or social conventions, is trying to force me into applying terms that don't suit the case? Conversely, can I be what I feel myself to be if the dominant language doesn't help me to construct it within myself, to give it my own voice? Caliban hated Prospero, but *The Tempest* implies that Sycorax's son didn't fully understand his hatred until his tormentor had given him a language of curses.

This leads to the third, and most important, word – love. There isn't much sense of it in these versions of his story; it tends to be smothered by anxieties about sex and male conformity, with the result that the myth is obsessed with the bedroom, but more or less blind in the matters of the heart. Yet these matters need to be placed at the centre of any interpretation. It's been seen how Clift's relationships, with men and women, sexual or otherwise, were fundamentally unsatisfactory. In fact, this writer has a sneaking suspicion that the actor wasn't the greatest lay north of Mott Street; he comes across as a man in need of emotional sustenance as much as sex. The issue is, however, what he wanted that sustenance, that love, to be. The evidence suggests that he didn't have a clue. He was a Caliban searching for his personal language of love, and he needed a Prospero to give him a voice.

Today, we have these Prosperos, even though their language is a kind of university rococo. For example, here is the American academic Marjorie Garber, in *Vice Versa: Bisexuality and the Eroticism of Everyday Life* (1995), on bisexuality as a liquefying definition: 'It is, then, an identity that is also *not* an identity, a sign of the uncertainty of ambiguity, the stability of instability, a category that defies and defeats categorization.' Stretching behind these rather intimidating words are the massed ranks of feminism, post-Stonewall gay rights and all the assaults they have made on the established conventions. The world has become more elastic, in certain circles at any rate.

Clift didn't have these weapons at his disposal: none existed; there was only an inner silence. It was nigh on impossible for him, therefore, to define and give voice to the complex forces that made up his version of loving and being. His self-articulacy can't have been helped by the emotional deprivation of his childhood. The evidence of this early life is lost, but, applying the principles of Alice Miller's *Thou Shalt Not Be Aware: Society's Betrayal of the Child* (1985), it's possible to see him as a man gazing into a mirror, which has been clouded by inadequate parenting; Sunny's life-denying ways didn't affirm the uniqueness of his being; given his particular emotional state, that uniqueness, the relationship between different forces and desires, would have been complicated. All this means that he didn't have an inner object or image, a sense of his feeling speaking clearly to himself. In Miller's view, artists as various as Samuel Beckett, Gustave Flaubert and Franz Kafka suffered from a similar lack; she believes that their writing was a substitute object, a way of working through the problem. Appropriately enough for our man, this process is central to a certain kind of acting. To understand why, we need to ponder the healing power of imagery itself, and thereby hangs a tale, from about A.D. 1 to A.D. 8, to be exact.

It goes like this. Bisexuality, says Marjorie Garber, 'by its very "existence" unsettles ideas about priority, singularity, truthfulness, and identity, it provides a crucial paradigm for thinking differently about human freedom.' The quotation marks round 'existence' suggest that we are in a linguistic minefield. Garber attempts to define the word further, though, by the use of an image, that of Tiresias in Ovid's *Metamorphoses*. As every schoolchild used to know, Tiresias came across two snakes copulating in a copse, and struck them with his staff. At once, he was cursed and was turned into a woman. Seven years later, he encountered the same snakes, hit them as before, and was returned to his original maleness. Thus, when the gods Juno and Jove were arguing about whether men or women received the most pleasure from sex, they called on Tiresias to adjudicate, because, as Ovid puts it, '[h]e knew both sides of love'. When Tiresias finds for Jove, however, the angry Juno blinds the man, but, in compensation, her partner gives the poor man the gift of prophecy, and, though no one could have foreseen it at the time, a highly prized guest appearance in *The Waste Land*. Garber finds the tale a useful metaphor because it encapsulates a host of questions about the fluid nature of certain identities. The image of what she calls a 'shape shifter' can encapsulate, and hold in balance, many seeming contradictions. It makes possible the expression of a state of being that can't be defined using conventional language.

This leads us, a little circuitously, to the psychological contexts surrounding the world of what might loosely be termed the 'performing arts'. One of the reasons why those who are gay, or who, in Clift's case, possess an element of gayness, flock to this world isn't a simple matter of fascination with camp or artifice. It's rooted in the psychological need to question, through creativity, the orthodox assumptions about the relationship between surface and essence, and hence between sexuality and gender, all the forces that trap and distort gay feeling, and that make self-articulacy so difficult. Actors, in particular, can't operate adequately in this work without some kind of aid to self-definition, an inner image, which can play with the problems surrounding seeming and being, and offer potential solutions to them. Simon Callow, the gay actor, writer and director, has written eloquently about this, even if the theme is implicit.

In Being an Actor (1984), he describes his training at the Drama Centre in London in the 1970s. During his early days, a psychic or emotional block frustrated him during the long hours of improvisation in class; try as he might, he couldn't get his feelings to flow. 'Emotions began to well,' he says, 'but then, at the crucial moment, some inner clamp sat on them, and though I whimpered somewhat, it remained a trickle, not a torrent.' The breakthrough came in an exercise when he was playing the role of a man who comes home to find his girlfriend in bed with someone else. After a few failed attempts to get to the emotional core of the scene, all his frustration burst forth; he became a maniac. The experience, which among other things involved the destruction of a three-seat settee, taught him a lesson. 'At a stroke,' he says, 'the mask that I had screwed to my face fell away.' He discovered 'a pool of liberated energy', which 'transform[ed] the brain, the head and the body – I was as one re-born'. Here was the psychological transformation that he needed, the discovery, through acting, of a personal centre. It was something more than mere impersonation. 'The problem was,' he reflects, 'that I thought the suit of armour, the mask, SIMON CALLOW, *were* my centre. I had sung songs, impersonated animals, donned garments, adopted accents; but it was always something that I imposed on top of what I was, always something I was DOING TO MYSELF, instead of letting it do me.'

These extracts are suggestive, not only because of their almost evangelical quality, but also because of their paradoxical pattern of feeling. Callow implies that a false self, as he understood it, is a mask that needed to be unscrewed, Dumas-like, in order for him to feel the truth and depth of his real being. Yet, at the same time, this re-birth, as he calls it, exists outside him in the transcendent sense of 'letting it do me'. The overall response, in fact, is magical, even religious (isn't the Holy Spirit supposed to 'do us'?). The art of acting is a form of homecoming in which, like the Tiresias myth, irreconcilables are reconciled in a revelatory way.

Callow presents this experience in isolation: he doesn't ask whether the narrative context of the improvisation had any influence on his Pauline conversion; he believes that the weeks of frustration, and humiliation at the hands of his teacher, were the main cause. Nevertheless, he is one of the rare actors who have tried to define the psychological and spiritual elements of their art. Most important of all, he suggests that acting, when it's working at top pressure, is both a flight from conventions, traditional language and the limitations they impose, and a journey into the depths of (it's hard to avoid this word) the soul. It's possible to see how such a fragmentary creature as Montgomery Clift could have tried, without any of Callow's self-awareness, to launch a similar project. After all, Tiresias was blind, but he had the gift of prophecy; he could see in other ways. Did Clift search for Tiresias in his work, and, if so, how? More to the point, could he, given his circumstances and times? These questions reveal new perspectives about his career and his intent.

The Elusive Butterfly

When Robert LaGuardia evokes the image of Clift alone at his desk, sifting through scripts, agonising and dithering, he is presenting a picture of the psychological and professional inertia that seems to have gripped the star during the great silence of 1953 to 1956. This is an accurate portrayal as far as it goes, but its implications need to be handled with care, because LaGuardia's image is a narrative device, part and parcel of his general biographical intent. It suggests that Clift is a conscience-wracked artist, grappling with inner demons that are fundamentally sexual, and it assumes, above all, that he is alone and oppressed. This leaves out the possibility that the star isn't merely passive, battling in the isolation of his personal closet, but reaching out and struggling with the dominant language that encases him, with the world at a particular point in history. The question is whether that language was sufficiently malleable for him to be able to bend it to his own, Tiresian purposes.

There is evidence to suggest that this is precisely what he tried to do; he was attempting to find a clearing for himself within a forest of questions raised by the culture of his time. Those questions were, and still are, wide and deep. They concern the yearning for artistic autonomy in a culture where commercialism and industrial processes compromise the attempt. Clift is said to have admired writers, and he was friendly with a few, Arthur Miller being the most notable. Yet, unlike writers, actors can only exercise their art in an arena that is influenced by agents, directors, executives, profit versus loss, the whole cacophony of the market place. A writer can soar alone, unpublished perhaps, but the work can nevertheless exist. Actors don't have that privilege. They need a commercial and logistical life support machine if their art is to come into being at all.

This is as true of theatre as it is of films, and the tension is inherent in the new, mass arts that came to prominence in the last century. Sinatra, for example, could portray himself as the *My Way* man, self-determining, free of the compromises of most industrial wage slaves, even though he couldn't have existed without the very corporate structures that he claimed to have escaped. In his case, however, the paradox was beneficial: it sustained the illusion; it gave him his excitement and edge. Clift may have worked within the same context, but he was closer to those doomed American artists, like Fitzgerald or Hemingway, who slipped through the gap between art and commerce, between being an artist and being a celebrity, and thus found themselves exposed to the snipers in no-man's land. This is an American as well as a psychological or sexual problem. Clift's ambitions, and his personal defeat, are rooted as much in the complexities of a continent as in the haunted wood of his own being.

★

By European standards, America is young. Only during the last century did it find both its unique voice, and, thanks to mass technologies, the ability to project that voice across the globe. When Clift was growing up in the 1920s, young writers, like Fitzgerald and his Princeton chum, the critic Edmund Wilson, were hailing the decade as a golden time, Wilson, in particular, suggesting that American literature was freeing itself from the New England Puritanism that had been dominant since the nineteenth century. In the theatre, too, playwrights and actors were challenging the old, European way of doing things; the 'little theatre' movement, the granddad of what was to become 'off-Broadway', was a forcing house for a specifically American form of drama. (Eugene O'Neill is the most famous example). As a result, commercial and experimental theatre worked side by side, with the Theatre Guild, for example, bringing more challenging work to the Great White Way. The Depression, however, put stresses on this relationship. The young, or youngish, began to question their country's belief in free enterprise and looked to radical politics, and to Stalin's Russia, for a solution to the economic crisis. The 1930s were the time of Roosevelt's New Deal, of worker's theatre projects, and of the Group Theatre, an offshoot of the Theatre Guild, whose tyro directors – Harold Clurman, Elia Kazan, Stella Adler and Lee Strasberg – were trying to create more authentic American theatre, politically and artistically. It was a turbulent period, but it was also an era of high ideals. More than today, New York was the hub of American cultural and intellectual life. Living and working there put one right at the heart of that drama, at the centre of those dreams.

Clift's biographers haven't given enough consideration to what this world meant for a young man of his limited background and eccentric education. Apart from an unsuccessful, and brief, attendance at the Dalton School in New York City in 1936 to 1937, he never went to school, nor was he exposed to the rough and tumble of university life. In consequence, his early career was his school or college, where he gained the kind of experiences that most young men of his age would have had long before. It was an elite education, too. From the start, Clift mainly worked on Broadway, with only a few humbler jobs in summer stock: he never had to trudge around the sticks, taking any old job and getting by on technique alone; as in his childhood, he was privileged yet deprived of many experiences that would have been helpful in later life. This helps to explain, in part, why his career has a hermetic quality, a lack of professional brio, as if he were in an expectant state, waiting for the visitation of an angel. As Simon Callow notes of Charles Laughton's similarly lucky beginnings, Clift never seems to have understood the get-on-and-do-it nature of some acting work, because everything he did was written in personal code, and his stage work defined the nature of what that code was.

Clift's career really got going, in terms of regular work, in 1938 when he featured in a number of ephemeral productions that were the standard fare of the commercial theatre of the time. Nineteen-forty, however, brought an important breakthrough when he landed a prestigious role in *There Shall Be No Night*, the production that introduced him to Phyllis Thaxter. This play, written by Robert E. Sherwood, who had been a pacifist during the 1930s, was a polemical piece designed to wake up America to the evils of totalitarian Europe and to the moral weakness of isolationism. The script may seem turgid to modern readers, but it had a great impact at the time (it won the Pulitzer Prize for Drama), especially because it starred the royal couple of Broadway, Alfred Lunt and Lynne Fontanne. The show ran for a hundred and eighty-one performances in New York and toured forty-six other cities; a second tour was planned, but the bombing of Pearl Harbour changed the political situation and it came to nothing. Even so, the play marked a significant change in Clift's fortunes. By the spring of 1942, he was appearing in *Mexican Mural*, an off-Broadway production directed by Robert Lewis, who was part of the Group Theatre, and a leading light in the Actor's Studio after the war. The production, which only lasted for a handful of performances, was one of the many attempts to create an artistic, rather than a commercial, company; although it failed, it led Clift into more adventurous territory. Later that year, he played the rebellious teenager, Henry Antrobus, in Thornton Wilder's *The Skin of Our Teeth*, a mythical saga of the human race's capacity to survive in a turbulent world. After that, Clift featured in a revival of Wilder's *Our Town* and then, in April 1944, he had a major role in Lilian Hellman's unfortunately titled *The Searching Wind*. This indictment of appeasement ran for three hundred and twenty-six performances, garnering the Critics' Circle Award for the best play of the season.

After this, Clift gained his first starring role, as a war-haunted young man in a minor production, *Foxhole in the Parlour*, before he starred alongside Edmund Gwenn (Kris Kringle in *Miracle on 34th Street*, 1947) in *You Touched Me!*, a piece of whimsy by Tennessee Williams and Donald Windham. The play had been staged to cash in on the success of Williams' first hit, *The Glass Menagerie*. The playwright never thought much of this bagatelle about a lieutenant in the Royal Canadian Air Force who breaks down the inhibitions of a sea captain's shy daughter; he left it out of his collected works. For Clift, it marked the end of an era. He wasn't to return to the stage for nearly ten years.

These main stage roles, however, coming as they do in such a formative period in the young actor's life, are vital in assessing his intent; they weren't merely his apprenticeship in his craft, but also the first draft of what he was later to attempt on film. They also help to explain why he was so choosy about his roles. For Clift wasn't a star egotist in the clichéd sense. Rather, as a literate, though sporadically educated man, he seems to have been searching for something deeper and bigger than the part itself, for a specific pattern, a pressure, which gave the character a unique quality. These stage performances have long since vanished, but his three long-running successes – *There Shall Be No Night*, *The Skin Of Our Teeth* and *The Searching Wind* – still moulder away in old books, and they offer detailed evidence.

As might be expected for an actor in his twenties, Clift's major roles during this period emphasise youth. Yet, given the times, his young men resonate with the particular needs and sacrifices of war. In his first hit, *There Shall Be No Night*, he plays Erik Valkonen, the idealistic son of a Finnish scientist (Alfred Lunt) and an American mother (Lynne Fontanne). As the Russians invasion of Finland edges towards their Helsinki home, husband and wife are faced with the question of whether they should make the moral and spiritual commitment to resisting evil. Robert Sherwood uses the play to condemn a world whose scientific advances, he believes, have made it complacent and lazy. Erik, the core narrative figure, is the conscience of the story; he rouses his father to his duty as a Finn, and his mother to her contrasting American heritage as a warrior for freedom. The character, in fact, is torn between his love for his parents and his belief that they must become as engaged in the crisis as he is. For instance, when the young man's fiancée accuses him of failing to understand his mother, he points out that, on the contrary, he understands something that she has forgotten, the fact that Americans have always ridden into battle in the cause of freedom and their beliefs: 'Americans fought for that same thing – for the same reason – the same need, that was in their souls. It was Americans who taught the whole world that it was *worth* fighting for!' Eventually the young man goes off to war and is killed, a tragedy that helps to change his father's heart: Dr Valkonen goes to the front as a medic. At the end of the play, with both son and husband dead, the widow and bereaved mother reads the doctor's final letter. 'Now – the death of our son is only a fragment in the death of our country,' he writes. 'But Erik and the others who give their lives are also giving to mankind a symbol – a little symbol, to be sure, but a clear one – of man's unconquerable aspiration to dignity and freedom and purity in the sight of God'. The curtain falls on what we would now call a feel-good note, with a weighty, and vague, sermon echoing in the audience's ears.

Erik isn't the largest part in Sherwood's play, but the brave, doomed, if unctuous boy is still a flashy pirouette, ideal for a young actor hoping to get noticed. Even so, the role is more than just an attraction-grabbing turn. For Erik is caught in the complex crosscurrents eddying between his love for his parents, his mother in particular, and what he believes to be the truth. In terms of the narrative structure, he starts out as a visionary, then later becomes a spiritual presence whose death turns him into a disembodied idea that reverberates throughout the play. His meaning resides in his extinction and sacrifice; he is both trapped and transcendent. This isn't to suggest that the play is a forgotten masterpiece: it isn't; the writing is heavy-handed and abstract. Nevertheless, in the context of Clift's career, it's a template for a lot that was to follow.

The Skin of Our Teeth was his next big hit. Here, he plays a teenager, who, unlike the rest of his family, is violent, dangerous, and hates his father; his big scene is a confrontation with the older man. There is nothing transcendent here, but there is a sense of entrapment and anger, of youth caught in a web spun by the older generation. This web is also present in *The Searching Wind*. Clift is a diplomat's son, who is convalescing at home, having been wounded in the leg while fighting in Italy. For most of the play, he seems peripheral to the action, just a character hanging around while his parents debate their own moral failure to oppose appeasement and to confront the problem of a long-standing love affair between the diplomat and his wife's best friend. Only at the end of the story, when the private and the public failures have been revealed, do we learn that the son's leg needs to be amputated. It's a neat Ibsenite piece of symbolism that is all of a piece with the tidy certainties, by modern standards, of the story as a whole. Now the son launches into his big speech. He condemns his parents, and, by implication, the America of the 1920s and '30s, for failing to get a moral grip: 'How do you say you like your country? I like this place.' Then he cries, 'And I don't want any more fancy fooling around with it. I don't want any more of Father's mistakes, for any reason, good or bad, or yours Mother, because I think they do it harm... I am ashamed of both of you, and that's the truth. I don't want to be ashamed that

way again. I don't like losing my leg. I don't like losing it at all. I'm scared –
but everybody's welcome to it as long as it means a little something and helps
to bring us out someplace. All right, I've said enough.'

Here again is a boy caught in a trap; once more, the emphasis is on youth in
an ethereal or even martyred sense. It's easy to see why Clift was effective in
these roles. Production stills show him as fragile, a little dreamy, and sexually
distant; the loveliness means something. In the early plays, this meaning was
the dilemma of idealistic youth, freeing itself from the prison of compromise
and failure to create a wider and deeper significance, even though a sacrifice
has taken place in the process.

The idea suggests an image: the butterfly escapes from its cocoon; the
metaphorical connections to Clift's childhood are obvious. Nevertheless, it's a
fragile concept, hard to sustain in the rough world of show business. To begin
with, as has been seen, it requires a particular form of narrative. Also, and the
biographies point this out, there is a Peter Pan element in the emphasis on
youth, which has the inevitable decay of ageing at its core. Clift was, in fact,
yet another example of the American artist who sees the world, and himself,
as an eternal prairie stretching into the distance with constant promise, but
who is incapable of facing the need to settle and mature. When that need does
arrive, though, the process is often regarded as tragic, like Fitzgerald, with his
sense that there will be tears after the boozy party, or of any exhausted and
prematurely dead rock and roll star you care to mention.

This tradition is more revealing in Clift's case than the 'Method actor' tag that
has rattled after him like tin cans behind a wedding car. For it makes sense of
the few statements he ever made about his craft. To take the 'Method' first: he
made only one recorded comment. Pointing out its roots in the theories of
the Russian acting guru, Constantin Stanislavsky, he noted that 'any good
actor uses the principles of Stanislavsky no matter what they [sic] do. It's a
marvellous thing for some poor slob who's in a hit – because he's playing that
role every night – and he's not expanding. Every time you find a truthful
actor, you find someone who bears out a little, not theories, but somehow the
realism that Stanislavsky battled to put on paper'. As the critic Ethan Mordden

has pointed out, Stanislavsky's theories (the 'Method' was Lee Strasberg's personal gloss on it) were a specifically theatrical approach, designed for the creation on stage of a work of art every night. The relationship to films is assumed to be there, but this is not at all clear. Moreover, by the time Clift attended Actor's Studio classes in 1947, his professional approaches were already established; he was only looking for the techniques that would affirm a position that was already set. His other statements on his craft, however, have a different and more constant theme, even though they were made during newspaper interviews, where a certain amount of hyperbole is part of the game. Talking at the time of *The Young Lions*, for example, he said, 'When I play a role I pour all my energy and emotion into it. My body doesn't know I'm only an actor. The adrenalin rushes around just like in a real emotional crisis when you throw yourself into an emotional scene. Your body doesn't know you're kidding when you become angry, tearful or violent for a part... I can't pace myself like other actors can'. This is quite a common line of copy, yet the references to the body, to the energetic and the physical, appear again and again in the interviews. Clift claimed that he didn't take the Marlon Brando role in *On the Waterfront* (assuming that he was offered it), because 'I just felt that I was physically wrong for the part. At no point could I envisage myself as a fighter. I haven't the physique for it.' Later, as middle age loomed, he told the show business writer Joe Hyams about his ambitions to direct: 'To be limited by my body is to be limited professionally. If the part of a sixteen year-old peasant fascinates you, you might not be able to play it, but you could direct it.' This is a curious concept – the director as controlling Svengali and invasive scoutmaster – but it shows how Clift saw his work in terms of youth and the appearance of youth. Other evidence confirms this. Jack Larson's mirror story ('I can still act') suggests the importance that the star attached to physicality; then there are tales about his reluctance to be filmed without his shirt (he was hairy); the actress Maureen Stapleton has an anecdote about suggesting he play a role in J. M. Synge's *The Tinker's Wedding*, which he rejected outright ('I can't play a blind old beggar'). The suggestion here, personal vanity apart, is that Clift was conscious of his beauty as a crucial aspect of his meaning, as if it were the key to his finding the centre, his own Tiresias. Clearly, this method involved ever-diminishing returns as the clock ticked. It was logical, then, to embrace film. Therefore, even if Clift partly took the *Red River* job because he needed the money, and partly, one suspects, for good old careerist reasons, one can't discount a desire to become eternal, like a text. Certainly, he seems to have embraced the medium wholeheartedly. By doing so, however, he found himself in a bind. Are film stars, and actors, different types of being? On screen, in factory-produced product, what exactly is art? In tracing his career from 1946 on, we are studying a man with an uncertain sense of these problems. Self-absorbed, grappling with the complexities of his upbringing and his own, narrow vision of how he can re-make himself through acting, he makes decisions that are like badly judged lunges in the dark.

In terms of 'art', if you like, the move from stage to screen was a mistake. For, in heading out west with Hawks and John Wayne in 1946, Clift in effect abandoned Broadway at the very moment when new, vital voices, like those of Tennessee Williams, Arthur Miller and William Inge, were beginning to make an impact. In consequence, he unwittingly rejected the opportunities that could have helped him to attain his vision. It was unfortunate, too, that just as he missed the boat in the theatre, he merely jumped on the sinking ship that was the Hollywood studio system. He was pulled down by the vortex of cultural and industrial change. In fact, with the wisdom of hindsight, it's easy to see that he shouldn't have become a film star in the first place.

'Film star', in this context, means the kind of creature that had become an integral part of the studio system. In 1946, that system looked secure. The 1920s and '30s had been a period of alarms and excursions, of mergers and bankruptcies, until, at the outbreak of the Second World War, the industry had resolved itself into five major corporations, each of which dominated production, distribution and exhibition; they were all part of major theatre chains. Next in the hierarchy were the companies that made films and gained screen time through distribution and exhibition deals with the conglomerates; what remained were bucket shop B-film operations, scrabbling for what they could on low budgets and small revenues. The guiding principle of this system, which helped to standardise product in a world where audiences were fickle and where the factories had to churn out about one film a week, was the genre (western, musical, whatever), and the star. These golden human beings, however, weren't a solid guarantee. As today, their popularity could rise and fall with an alarming swiftness, and some performers, too, had the irritating habit of resisting what studio heads regarded as economically beneficial typecasting. Like it or not, though, studios needed stars. In 1949, for example, Metro-Goldwyn-Mayer, the most glittering production house of them all, had eighty men, women, children and a dog (Lassie) tied to long-term contracts. This meant that the star was bound hand and foot to the corporation, and, more to the point, to a financial deal that made them company property, so they couldn't go cherry-picking among the opposition and thereby raise prices. Clift had turned down one of these MGM seven-year contracts in 1941. If he had accepted it, he might have ended up like other MGM pretty boys – Tom Drake, Van Johnson, Peter Lawford – whose sole purpose seems to have been to show off the efforts of the wardrobe department and to act opposite June Allyson without visibly wincing.

When Clift reached Hollywood, however, this security, which had been bolstered by bumper revenues during the war years, was coming to an end. One reason was that leisure patterns were about to change. This didn't just mean the arrival of television, but the shift of the population away from the big urban areas, where many cinemas were located, to the suburbs, to the rich fields of the consumerist dream. Another reason was that the politicians weren't happy with the conglomerates; they believed they were running a stitch-up operation designed to keep the competition subservient. There had been rumblings of discontent in the 1930s, but it was only after the war that the battles for the screen began with the so-called Paramount Decree of 1948. This stipulated that exhibition had to be separated from production and distribution; in effect, it began to create a market where films were made and screened on a picture-by-picture basis. The year of the decree also saw the release of *The Search* and *Red River*. Clift became a star at the very moment when the whole game was about to change.

With this, as with the theatre, he had bad luck made worse by weak judgement. In essence, Clift worked as a freelance, not in the way that made sense in the late 1940s and early 1950s, where a director like Hawks, or an actor like Cary Grant, moved from studio to studio in a series of package deals for so many films, but as a gun for hire, grabbing what jobs he could. By the middle of the decade, when the studio system was well down the slippery slope, stars (James Stewart is an early example) worked on deals that offered them high fees, percentages and the kind of clout enjoyed by the multi-million dollar celebrities of our own time. Once again, Clift fell between the two systems. He didn't enjoy the consistent attention of one studio, which, though it could restrict an artist, still had a vested interest in developing him or her, but neither did he have the advantages of the new world.

This is odd, because, from about 1949 until the early 1960s, the presiding genius of the star's career was Lew Wasserman, the Genghis Khan of the Music Corporation of America; this early example of the super agent was a central figure in the establishment of that new Hollywood world. As Connie Tuck has shown, Wasserman and MCA were prime forces in the replacing of the dying studio contract system with the agency package deal (they did the business for James Stewart, for example): she suggests that the agent was a visionary and a shark, or a sharkish visionary, eating up everything and everyone; he danced with the devil of illegality, and, like a Faustus who never had to pay the price, ended up as the lord of Universal Studios. In theory, then, Clift had a king maker on his side. (His actual agent was a minion, Jay Kantor, but Tuck shows that every employee was compelled to follow Lew's aggressive policies.) In practice, as we have seen, MCA sent him piles of material, which he fiddled with and then rejected. It's as if he were mesmerised by two stark choices. On the one hand, he could be a film star, and keep himself consistently in front of the mass public, or, on the other, he could be a more traditional actor, where Broadway, more than Hollywood, was the logical place to be. Yet he fudged the decision. Instead, he dithered, remaining with film (except for one brief theatrical diversion in 1954), but never quite seeming happy with it. We can see, then, that in industrial terms, Clift wasn't just a rebel battling within the system, a kind of counter star as he is sometimes painted, but more an unstar, suspended between different intents and possibilities. As a result, the man Barney Hoskyns calls the 'Beautiful Loser' isn't wholly the tragic and doomed victim of the myth. If there is a tragedy, then it lies in his inability to apply judgement and to chart a firm course. To coin a phrase, he lost himself in show business.

If one looks at the overall shape of Clift's film career, at the nature of his roles, at their narrative structures and the circumstances of their production, it becomes clear that, except for a few outstanding examples (*A Place in the Sun*, say, or *From Here to Eternity*), they failed his inner vision. They didn't provide, not sufficiently at least, the specific narrative context in which he wanted to exercise his craft. This is shown both in the films he chose (as much as a freelancer can choose anything) and in the vacillations of his career as a whole.

★

Clift assaulted film stardom with a double-pronged attack that was a result of the vagaries of distribution rather than of any direct intention. *The Search*, released in 1948, is the lachrymose story of a little boy, a Czech refugee, looking for his mother in the wreckage of post-war Europe; he is helped in his quest by a kindly American GI (Clift), who unofficially adopts the boy and plans to take him to the States, until Mother turns up in the final tear-stained minutes. As Judith M. Kass has shown in her survey of Clift's films, his role, though substantial, is peripheral to the main quest. (In fact, it's never resolved; boy embraces mother, while the soldier's reaction is never explored. The film just dumps him.) Nevertheless, the part gave Clift his first Oscar nomination for Best Actor, *The Search* being one of those clichéd issue pictures that are impressive at the time, but that lack any inner life to give them greater longevity. By contrast, *Red River*, which was shot in 1946 but not released for two years thanks to distribution delays and a legal case, was a super western, a Howard Hawks enterprise, which meant that it was designed to make more money and reach more theatres with greater publicity. (It did both; Hawks was the artist as a patrician huckster.) Thus, 1948 was a double for Clift: he enjoyed a commercial hit, which made him an object of teenage drooling; then there was the prestige success, something that was more 'artistic' and 'serious'. In the short term, this duality was an advantage; it made him special. In the studio system of the time, however, it also indicated an anomaly in the long term. For Clift was neither a John Wayne, a star tied to certain box office genres, nor a theatre actor who brought an air of Broadway legit to the vulgar sound stage. Hence, the new star wasn't easy to classify, a problem that wasn't helped by his fastidiousness in choosing roles. At first, a three-picture deal with Paramount, arranged by Wasserman, solved the problem. The first film in his contract was *The Heiress* (1949), an elegant, careful adaptation of a stage version of Henry James' *Washington Square* (1880), directed by the elegant and careful William Wyler. Here, Clift plays Morris Townsend, an impecunious young man who courts Catherine Sloper, the homely heiress of the title. This being the late 1940s, the nearest the studio could get to plainness was Olivia de Havilland with an unflattering hairdo; the story revolves round whether Morris really loves the hairdo, or is only hungering after the money that it represents. As with his previous two films, Clift isn't so much the lead as the human lacunae round which the narrative revolves; he is like the murderer who needs to be unmasked in a detective thriller, although, in this case, he murders his own heart as much as Catherine's. The role has some of the flashy qualities of Clift's star turns on Broadway. This is about all that can be said too for his portrayal of a young airman in *The Big Lift* (1950), an appallingly self-righteous tale of the Berlin airlift, romance, betrayal and the American way. After this non-event, which nevertheless gave him an all-too-rare chance at a little light comedy, it was back to Paramount for *A Place in the Sun*, the second film under his contract, and his breakthrough as an artist on film.

As Graham McCann notes, this show, which is a version of Theodore Dreiser's novel *An American Tragedy* (1925) but with the social significance filtered out, was the first Clift film to establish him as a 'rebel' star; whatever its limitations in the eyes of modern viewers, it fixed his context, his 'vulnerability', 'ambiguity', 'sensitivity'. Moreover, this time the story is definitely centred on him. He plays George Eastman, a young man from a poor background who is given a job in a relative's factory, and is faced with the choice of marrying Alice Tripp, a woman from a similar background, who he has got pregnant (played by Shelley Winters at her petulant best), or ditching her in favour of the rich man's daughter (Elizabeth Taylor, and she was never lovelier). The Clift character gains its power both from the social pressure, which belabours him with needs and desires that it won't let him fulfil, and from the dream of glamour, wealth and freedom as embodied in Liz's well-dressed curves. Another layer of interest lies in the problem of whether Alice dies in a genuine boating accident or whether Clift has helped her on her way. Directed by George Stevens, the film has the sleek hysteria of

'REAL BUTTERFLY POSSIBILITIES.'
ALFRED HITCHCOCK AND MONTGOMERY CLIFT ON THE SET OF *I CONFESS* IN 1953.

the period; it yearns for deeper meaning, but, in the end, as McCann says, has to make do with sex. It's this portrayal of a man's sexual and social desires, trapped between opposing forces, which established Clift as something more than a beautiful leading man with a gift for reticent elegance. There is an edginess in his work here. The role required him to search and dream, to melt and reconstruct his identity even though the process was self-defeating. He was both cramped and soaring. When, at the end of the film, a court condemns him to death, there are no Sydney Carton-style heroics. A little like Albert Camus' *Outsider*, he has done what he has done because he is who he is. This complexity was unusual for 1950s Hollywood. It speaks of a new elasticity in its portrayal of a man and of America. More crucially, from Clift's point of view, it suggested creative possibilities for the future, if the gods were kind.

At first, they were positively generous: the actor received his second Academy Award nomination for this performance. Yet, as we saw in the contemporary journalism, neither the studios nor the reporters knew what to make of him. A less hesitant and uncertain star, or one labouring under the well-manicured thumb of a studio boss, might have kept himself in front of the public by seeing the film game for what it was and turning up in standard product in the hope that the law of averages would throw up a few worthwhile projects. Yet Clift seems always to have been searching for that elusive butterfly, first glimpsed when he worked with the Lunts; his choice of roles after the breakthrough of *A Place in the Sun* indicates that he wasn't that interested in film stardom as such, but rather in the self-realisation that it could represent. (All the same, this didn't stop him from exploiting his privileged position, demanding that Rostova accompany him on set, or, ably abetted by a good agent, playing the money game.) His next project, for example, had real butterfly possibilities. *I Confess* (1953) is the story of a young Roman Catholic priest, who, via the confessional, discovers the identity of a murderer, but can't reveal his secret without compromising the confidentiality of his office. It also happens that, before he took the cloth, our hero had an affair with a married woman (Anne Baxter), who was being blackmailed by the murder victim. Clift has a motive, then, and, worse, no alibi, so the story revolves round the question, should he save himself or stay true to his vocation? The original idea was that the priest would eventually go the way of George Eastman, a more compelling ending than the one that got filmed. (It involves a court revelation, a chase, and the death of the real murderer; you know the sort of thing.) The potential for Clift's brand of knotted romanticism is clear; moreover, with Alfred Hitchcock as director, the chance for a good film lay within reach. In the end, though, the story is a bore, with Clift looking as daft as Frank Sinatra in *The Miracle of the Bells* (1948) and given no opportunity to explain why he is going round looking so conscience-stricken all the time. (Hitchcock has been criticised for failing to articulate the specific Roman Catholic dilemma in his protagonist, but the problem isn't solely the director's or the script's. Clift was a Quaker, thanks to Sunny; his facial blankness may be due, in part, to an inability to connect intellectually with the frills and the popery.) Whatever the case, *I Confess* was a disappointment, and now Clift turned to another film with a major director at the helm. This was called, in the American version at least, *Indiscretion of an American Wife* (released USA 1954), directed by Vittorio De Sica and extensively buggered up by its producer, David O. Selznick. Starring the mogul's then wife, Jennifer Jones, it was intended as a vaguely neo-realist study, a tale of a married woman parting with her lover at the Stazione Termini in Rome, interwoven with vignettes of other waiting passengers. One can see why Clift was attracted to a story in which romance was only one strand of a more complex, more human tapestry; after an agonised shoot, however, with Selznick driving De Sica mad with his infamous memos, disillusionment soon settled in. Hacked to bits for its American release, the show is little more than *Brief Encounter* with added cappuccino; the editing is so clumsy that it's remarkable De Sica kept his name on the credits. Luckily for Clift, it wasn't released until after his next job, *From Here to Eternity* (1953). There will be a lot more to say about this film, which marks the high point of his achievement and his dream. For the moment, though, only three things need to be said. First, he was nominated again for the best actor Oscar. Secondly, he failed to get it. Thirdly, he sank into a deep depression, and the result was the great three year silence.

We are back to LaGuardia's image of the agonised man in his study; it's worth pausing now, like Clift, and chewing our lower lips. What was going on? Here is a man with a very specific, even narrow, concept of what he wants to achieve. The majority of the early work doesn't really fulfil it. Even so, at the very moment when he reaches some approximation of the desire with *A Place in the Sun*, he gets lumbered with indifferent Hollywood work. The next step, turning to Europe, was logical: the actor had spent so many years there; it had a tradition of 'artistry'. Alas, Selznick, the mogul as wrecker, mangled that idea, and *From Here to Eternity*, which was a critical and commercial triumph, nevertheless failed to come up with an Oscar for its leading man. Fred Zinnemann told Maurice Leonard that the roulette of the ballot box played its part: both Clift and his co-star Burt Lancaster were up for the statuette, but this split the vote, and the award eventually went to William Holden for his role as Sergeant J. J. Sefton in Billy Wilder's prisoner of war thriller, *Stalag 17* (1953). A more pragmatic man might have put this down to the luck of the draw and to the usual political game that attends these affairs. Unfortunately, Clift was an idealist, an insecure one at that, and there is evidence to suggest that his failure to win the gong created a crisis of self-belief. 'What do I have to do to prove I can act?' he wailed to a journalist on Oscar night; during the following days, LaGuardia has him locked away in despair. It seems, therefore, that the Academy Award represented a hunger for affirmation, and, when it didn't occur, the actor stopped, agonised, and ruminated to an almost morbid degree. Then, even while he was debating what he wanted his films to be, and how he was to live in future on screen, another change of direction came to mind. It was time to go back to the stage, after nine long years.

Clift's return to theatre, at this moment of career jitters, is a poignant episode in his life. While he had been away, Miller and Williams had come to the fore, but the actor chose not a new play, but a classic, *The Seagull*, which, tellingly perhaps, had last been produced on Broadway by the Lunts. The whole affair seems to have been an amateur shambles. To begin with, Clift had been the sort-of-director; he had been working on it in a vague, workshop fashion with Kevin McCarthy, Maureen Stapleton and Mira Rostova. Yet, when the idea was picked up for an off-Broadway production, it wasn't for any bunch of highbrows who could be lured into a cramped basement. This was a production for the Phoenix Theatre, an ambitious company pursuing the cloudy dream of an American national theatre; its previous production had been *Coriolanus* starring Robert Ryan and directed by John Houseman, the former colleague of Orson Welles. Clift was playing, therefore, for high stakes, an indication of a need to establish a seriousness, an affirmed self, that Hollywood had failed to provide. Freedom from the factory, however, only confirmed that he wasn't the kind of star who can flourish with production responsibilities. Although there was a nominal director, Norris Houghton, one of the founders of the Phoenix, the performances were so out of kilter, and inaudible, that Arthur Miller had to be brought in to sort out the mess; moreover, Clift, at thirty-four or so, was getting a little long in the tooth to play one of Anton Chekov's soulful young Russians. Most depressing of all, spectators flocked to see a film star, but the critics left to write indifferent copy. Maybe Clift had wanted it too much in the first place.

When he returned to the camera, then, in 1956, it was another financial decision, although he didn't strike gold as he had with *Red River*. It's hard to work out why *Raintree County* (released 1957) is so awful. Apart from being an example of the widescreen epic, one of the dreariest genres cooked up by Hollywood to combat changing times, the film is a vapid romance swollen by the Civil War background and flatulent symbolism. Bosworth claims that the pre- and post-crash Clift are discernible, but, in fact, his whole performance is numb. Too old to play a young Yankee with dreams of literary glory, and too intelligent to engage with the hack work that is the dialogue, he takes the wisest way out and disappears inside himself, while Elizabeth Taylor simply shrieks. (She is supposed to be a mad southern belle, but the racket is a response as much as a performance.) Commercially, the farrago did well enough, but, more than the car crash, which took place during the shooting, this costume horror marks the actor's career descent from young lead to middle-aged character player.

In the ensuing, epilogue years, we see a different Clift; his roles may have a butterfly potential, but, like him, their wings are tattered. The role in *The Young Lions* (1958), his first full job since the crash, isn't much more than an extended cameo, albeit subtly and feelingly executed, while all that follows is either a half-hearted attempt to breathe life into dead material (*Lonelyhearts* (1959) is more than dead; it's a mummification of Nathanael West's novella), or a lunge at a possibility that is rarely fulfilled. In this way, *The Misfits* (1961) is the triumph of a good actor responding to decent material, while *The Defector* (1966), his last film, shows what dross might have awaited him if he had lived, and if his bank manager, and the industry, had proved unsympathetic. It's just possible that if he had survived to play Major Weldon Penderton in *Reflections in a Golden Eye* (1967), he would have uncovered in himself the anxieties that America itself was discovering, something anxious and conflicted, the life blood of the counter-culture. Equally, however, it could have been a dead-end. (The film that exists is merely Huston in his more bombastic mould, and Brando comes across as a man in urgent need of a herbal laxative.) Nevertheless, it would be an overstatement to paint Clift as the Hollywood equivalent of Richard Savage, the chaotic artist laid low by an unfeeling world and by his own weaknesses and gifts. The real problem is that his complexities lead him to demand too much from films, too much, indeed, from art itself. If we are left with fragments, or promises rather than a fully shaped achievement, then that is because most of life is like that.

★

So far, we have been looking at the life, or, to be more precise, the ways in which that life has been shaped into biography. This chapter has tried to show how Clift has been moulded in a particular way, and an alternative mould has been suggested. That leaves the problem of what he achieved in films. For LaGuardia, the effect is compelling, if vague: 'The public remembers him as a splendid screen presence, glamorous and vulnerable. It floats by on that giant screen, the image of the intensity of youth, in its most beautiful guise.' Graham McCann is a fully qualified scholar, but a certain wooziness grips him, too. The star was, he writes, 'rather remote, displaced, a loner, and somewhat androgynous in his appeal.... Inwardness, calculation, coolness and warmth – these were the qualities Clift embodied.' Right enough, but these comments assume that films simply transmit an essence; there is no sense of how viewers' responses are guided by the techniques of the medium, how meeting Clift on screen may not be a simple matter of 'the real' automatically transferring itself to 'the reel' (to adapt Samantha Barbas's phrase). We are back with language again, except that, this time, it's of a peculiarly cinematic kind.

The Wedding Before the Wooing

Stories about the early days of film are often suspect. One of the most questionable is the tale of the early audiences who saw footage of a steam train chugging towards them, and leapt from their seats in amazement, unable, the yarn suggests, to distinguish between the image on screen and the reality now standing at Platform Nine. On reflection, this interpretation of their response doesn't make sense. After all, the train would have been in black and white, it would have been soundless, or accompanied, perhaps, by piano music; moreover, like films today, the picture would have been in two dimensions. Those viewing pioneers can't have been gullible idiots. It's possible, then, that, if they jumped in surprise, this reaction was the result of a more complicated inner negotiation between what they knew a train to be, and what they were discovering about how a film could represent it. They were responding to a new way of seeing and showing, not confusing the picture with the thing pictured.

Since those early days, these questions have become even more complicated. Today, there are plenty of hard working academics turning an honest penny by studying how, in the modern, video-saturated environment, reality itself is questionable. We are the images that we consume, they argue, and, to a degree, the images consume us; meanwhile, sinister capitalists control the whole process, and their products define our very souls (which, by the way, we no longer have). This is a crude, and jaundiced, simplification. Still, it indicates how a star is a product of the very structure of film language. In fact, what Nick Carraway, the narrator of F. Scott Fitzgerald's *The Great Gatsby* (1925), says about that star-like hero is one of the most succinct statements on how the system operates. 'If personality is an unbroken series of successful gestures,' he writes, 'then there was something gorgeous about him, some heightened sensitivity to the promises of life, as if he were related to one of those intricate machines that register earthquakes ten thousand miles away.'

Without these 'gestures', there is no personality, gorgeous, or otherwise.

The linguistic game works along these lines. In the way that the characters in a novel are made up of words (Mr Micawber belongs to the texture of *David Copperfield*; he is only detachable in our imaginations), so a star is made up of shots, sounds, lighting and all the other elements that constitute the multi-media experience of a film. In consequence, big star moments, like Rhett and Scarlett's clinch against the sunset in *Gone With The Wind* (1939), are really distillations of everything that the film is communicating; this includes its structure, the balancing of social conventions and attitudes, the plastic qualities of movement and the play of light, the choices, and juxtapositions, created by editing. Still, the literary analogy only goes so far. For stars aren't created in our imaginations by words: they are specific images of particular human beings, like Sinatra with his tilted fedora, or John Wayne ambling across a desert; they are real only insofar as their gestures persuade us that they exist. How they look, move, and operate as devices within a film's narrative are the central elements of their meaning. These are the gestures that need breaking down into their constituent parts.

With Clift, as with many other stars, the most powerful weapon in his armoury is the way he looks. Those looks are beautiful. That high forehead, the sculpted nose, the small mouth that opens to reveal delicate teeth, are aspects of a physical type that wasn't common during his heyday, and is unusual even now. His face is best appreciated in the austerity of black and white; colour tends to overwhelm him, just as the wide screen (see *Raintree County* in particular) forces the camera to stand too far away, thereby diminishing his impact. As a result, he seems to be a creature that has strayed from the lost world of silent films, or from the later glory days of the divas, of Garbo or Dietrich. Like them, his face has a sculptural quality; like Marlene and Greta, too, he never sells us his sexuality, but is cool and veiled, luring us into his world. In this respect, he is a throwback to the days when stars were expected to convey an aristocratic distance. His roles may require him to play ordinary men − soldiers, impecunious outsiders − but the beauty partially undermines the democratic intent. He is like a prince in a Wildean fairy tale, wandering dreamily among the populous, disguised as a swineherd.

All this means that, as a narrative device, Clift doesn't communicate settled meanings: rather, he holds things in tension; he implies and doesn't show. Compare him with James Dean, who was a colour and wide-screen man in all three of his films, and who makes us as aware of his meaning as surely as if he had a neon sign, displaying 'Tortured Young Man', bolted to his head. In *East of Eden* (1955), for example, he does everything to make sure that his confusion, his lack of clarity, is as crystalline as possible. Aided by the magic letterbox, he shuffles, floppy as a puppet, pleads with his father using gestures that wouldn't have been out of place in Sir Henry Irving's Lyceum; there is even a scene where, standing on a swing, he swoops away from the lens and back again, the camera partly moving with him, as if his feeling can only be conveyed through hyperactivity. Dean is, in fact, a narcissist, so high on himself that one can imagine him looking in a mirror and succumbing to the sin of Onan. He pouts and preens; he is aware of his body like an eighteenth-century Macaroni was aware of his frills; even his hair is a little too thought-through. By contrast, Clift never comes on to the camera in Jimmy's fashion; he holds back and doesn't announce his meaning. Instead, he offers up evidence, which we have to work out using our own intelligence and sensibility. His successful gestures are small ones, but they suggest an Atlantis of submerged significance.

Look at him: he has a repertoire of concentrated techniques, which crop up in many of his films, irrespective of the role. One of the most eloquent is the use of his eyes; the detail of their movement, on the really big screens of his day, must have been as dramatic as a Peckinpah shoot-out. In many of his love scenes (*A Place in the Sun* and *I Confess* are good examples), he reworks the tired cliché of the leading man gazing soulfully into his female co-star's eyes. His own don't gaze at all; instead, they flicker and roam, from chin to mouth to forehead, giving the scene an urgency it might not otherwise have. The viewer senses that love is present, but it's not quite sexual; the eyes yearn, but possession doesn't seem to be the point. It's an unsettling device. Like Charles Laughton in some of his films, Clift seems to take the scene outside the boundaries of the usual Hollywood romance; in his case, he lures it to a place where glamour and beauty are the subjects of a pained idolatry. Those darting eyes are so restless, because they seem to be looking at a point beyond the woman, at some vision of Woman in general, in fact, and at the unfulfillable dream that She represents. Put another way, he is enacting a possibility as much as a relationship, and, in so doing, pushes the scene beyond the conventions. His eyes turn it into a question mark.

Another weapon in his arsenal, which has a comparable power, works in mid- or long-shot, rather than in close-up. This is the walking and thinking scene. One of the best is the build-up to the big confrontation in *Red River* when Clift heads out in the open air to face his nemesis, John Wayne, who has vowed to track him down and kill him. Without dialogue, only with the weight of our narrative expectations behind him, the younger star eases himself (there is no other word) across the screen. His body is liquid (as the critic Gerald Mast put it, he was 'refreshed' by Joanne Dru the night before; it shows). His hips sway; there is grace and no strain; his body has the rhetorical effectiveness of a dance. Watching him, we sense that this seemingly fragile figure has the moral, if not the physical strength of Wayne; the sight encapsulates the film's central relationship, and, as we shall see, the essence of its concerns. Clift pulls off this trick of concentration again and again, with different narrative emphases, depending on the film. For example, in *The Heiress*, there is a fine moment when Morris Townsend is left alone in one of the Washington Square rooms: we catch him wandering around, eyeing up the furniture and the knick-knacks. The director, William Wyler, is on record as saying that he wanted to capture the complexity of Maurice's motives. (He succeeded; in its own way, the film is even more oblique than Henry James' original novel.) As Morris moves like a smooth panther through the riches of Old New York, Clift communicates the whole duality of the film, the idea that he may want both the woman and her wealth, but isn't sure himself.

These two gifts, for revealing expression on the one hand, and for meaningful movement on the other, are Clift's great achievement; it's an intellectual, rather than a sexual power, but expressed through a sensual physicality. There is another way in which a gesture that is also a thought enhances his impact, and it brings to mind George Cukor's advice to Gavin Lambert about the importance of a director never allowing an actor to play a scene with the knowledge of what would happen next. Even in mediocre films, Clift is never tempted by this knowingness. In fact, he never plays a moment before it's appropriate, so that the 'intensity' so often mentioned by fans and writers can more accurately be described as an act of thinking: he plays a scene as if he were right there in the audience, not knowing what will happen himself. Both face and body are at work here, as can be seen in *From Here to Eternity*, where he is upstairs in a brothel (well, 'dance hall'; the Production Code still needed placating in 1953). He is telling Lorene (Donna Reed) about why he has consistently refused to box for his troop, even though he is being bullied for his refusal. In structural terms, the scene is little more than a dreary piece of Hollywood 'back story' in which every human action is required to have a discernible motive. Without ever breaking away from this aim, Clift's acting makes the scene richer and more complicated. Watch him, particularly his face and the way he uses his body. He hunches and frowns; the camera, holding him in a loose mid shot, enables him to act out an internal chamber drama when he reveals how he blinded a man in a previous fight, and, he implies, felt a subsequent remorse. At this point, the possibility for schlock is infinite; Clift avoids the trap, because he understands that the camera, like Gatsby, is an intricate machine that can register the most distant tremors. In this, he is like Louise Brooks in *Pandora's Box* (1929), that glory of the dying days of silent film when actors and directors had grasped the subtle force of movement and expression. In G.W. Pabst's film, Brooks can turn her head, frown, or smile, and make as big an impact as a heroine fleeing her fate in a D.W. Griffith melodrama. Clift uses the same approach. It's no coincidence that, like Brooks, he has a very beautiful neck.

All this reveals Clift's special way with the camera. Still, the microphone needs mentioning, too. As the *From Here to Eternity* brothel scene shows, Clift didn't have a conventionally good voice; there is a story that theatre audiences had trouble hearing him in *The Seagull*, and this is no surprise. In film terms, however, it's a persuasive instrument. Although the tone is thin, the accent a little anonymous, and the softness of the sibilants almost effete, it possesses, none the less, just the right tone for a sound track. This is because, being a light baritone, it rests easily in the ear, and, being insecure in the upper register, it can suggest hesitancy and vulnerability. Clift is well aware of this quality; he exploits his weaknesses, just as Sinatra used the thinner top notes in his singing to evoke that distinctive, bruised machismo. In his scene with Donna, Clift's song conveys an unmacho doubt; he is very different, in this respect, from the character in James Jones's original novel. He strings us along from word to word; we are held in suspense, because we are all too aware that the string might break. In consequence, this potentially banal scene has a resonance beyond its immediate function in the plot. We hear Clift reliving the experience of the injury in his mind; as he does so, a tenderness, an unstated love, is interpolated into the scene. It's as if there is something more at stake here than the blinding of Dixie Wells; a kind of male romance has been suggested. The biographies claim that the director, Fred Zinnemann, let Clift edit the script for this scene, but, whatever the actor's contribution, the achievement is the same. The star gives the sequence a rich, ambivalent life, which liquefies the conventions. His output contains many other examples, such as his duet with Marilyn Monroe in *The Misfits*, where, looking up at her with his battered face and his bandaged head, he describes the loss of his mother to his stepfather, and pleads for the younger woman's friendship.

It can be seen, then, that Clift is a master of cinematic language. Yet, thinking back to LaGuardia and McCann, mere technical mastery doesn't explain why they respond to him as a magical presence. The term 'ambiguity' matters here, because it indicates, although it doesn't pin down, the sense that Clift had an unorthodox quality, similar to the transgressive elements that worried his biographers. This word suggests, however, that there are fixed poles, created by objective laws, between which the ambiguous figure can oscillate; the implication is that these poles relate to gender or sexuality. As we saw earlier, this kind of judgement isn't helpful. We can get to the heart of Clift's meaning only if we discard grand ideas about the natural order of sexuality, and locate his achievement within the very texture of the films themselves. In this context, his looks matter in a quite superficial sense: beautiful, or even pretty, men can suggest sexual ambiguity, though this may say more about the desires of the viewer than the nature of the star. The deeper questions, however, relate to how we perceive the role of men and women on screen, particularly in 1950s films, and how the language of those films can shape our responses.

These issues are active in the big love scene between Clift and Elizabeth

Taylor in *A Place in the Sun*. It's no surprise that this sequence had a considerable impact at the time: its heightened eroticism, though dated, has some mileage in it even today. The moment of passion occurs at a party in a grand house; Clift and Taylor, whose interest in each other has already been established, take the opportunity to be alone together on the terrace outside. The film plays the scene in big close-ups, which aren't used at any other point in the whole story; to increase the tension, these shots are obscured now and then by one or other of the stars' shoulders, or part of their heads, so that the audience's feelings of closeness to the scene are complicated by a sense of other bodies obscuring the view; thus, the keynote is voyeurism, a sense of the illicit. At first glance, the roles of the man and the woman seem to be straightforward, because their appearance is conventional. Taylor is all woman, in the sense that she is dressed in high-class party fashion, while Clift is all suit and short back and sides, a chap straight out of an old *Saturday Evening Post* advertisement, but without the pipe. Yet the way in which the potential lovers act undermines how they seem, and this dislocation, along with the shooting style, gives the sequence an extra layer of unease. For, while both parties are tremulous and nervous, each swaps traditional gender sides, at least for some of the time: Clift is gentle, confused and yielding; Taylor is what our mothers would have called 'forward' (in fact, she also says 'tell mama, tell mama all' at one point, which destabilises the conventional roles further). In a limited way, then, the stars play with the received ideas of masculinity and femininity. Judged by the prevailing conventions of 1950s Hollywood, this is a breath of fresh air from a distant and uncharted territory.

This isn't the whole story, however; something important in terms of men and women happens within what might be called the very weave of the imagery itself. Because the film came out of the Paramount stable, it's shot in the discreet, glowing fashion that was a major element in the studio's house style, and this lighting (the photographer was William C. Mellor) heightens the beauty of both man and woman, never mind who is wearing the pants. In the animated shop window that is a Hollywood factory product, the management is, unconsciously perhaps, selling us the desirability of both sexes. Taylor is dark and silk-skinned, with those cow eyes and full lips that tempt us to imagine what it would be like to kiss them; he, being older, has fine lines on his forehead and down the side of his face; the bone structure is more pronounced than hers, and that small, slightly prissy mouth isn't a full-scale Hollywood come-on; kissing him, one imagines, might be regarded as impolite. Even so, beauty is before us; the image, in this glamorous instance, blesses them without favour. If this is a magical scene, then its excitement is rooted in the linguistic manipulations, so to speak, which have just been described. Clift's magic isn't merely emitted on screen, as if the technical apparatus of film story telling didn't exist. On the contrary, it's a product of that very apparatus, and of our relationship with it. We viewers are partly responsible for the magic, in fact, because our assumptions are being manipulated.

These questions of structure and reading are true of most films in most periods, but they are especially relevant to the Hollywood of the 1950s when the industry was in flux, along with the culture of which it was a part. So many films during this period (Clift's own *The Big Lift* is just one dispiriting example) aren't subtle narratives; they seem to enact a set of rigid preconceptions, particularly about the relationships between the sexes. In consequence, the shape of the story, the cutting and especially the performances have an ossified quality; little in their values is able to escape and breathe. If Clift strikes us today as special, then that is because he is doing something different within these conventions. This isn't to say that he works against the grain of a film, merely that he opens up greater possibilities.

One of those possibilities is love, emotionally and physically, between men. There are a number of ways in which a film can be seen as gay, but the most subtle method, the one that requires the maximum give and take between the viewer and the film, comes into play when its structure of values, and the sensibility of the spectator, are in continual, creative tension, so that the show seems to contain a potential that gay viewers can grasp and develop in parallel with what is ostensibly going on. The aim of the film isn't relevant; the question is whether its methods make this alternative view possible. When Clift first presented himself to audiences in a major commercial production, it's telling that he appeared in just such a film. For, whatever Howard Hawks thought he was up to, *Red River* is as gay as New Year's Eve.

'TAKE 'EM TO MISSOURI, MATT.'
JOHN WAYNE AND MONTGOMERY CLIFT IN *RED RIVER* (1948).

★

For those puritans who have never wasted their Saturday afternoons gawping at old black and white images on television, this film is an epic western, so epic that *Rawhide* (1959-1966), the television series that helped to establish Clint Eastwood's stardom, was able to spin out umpteen episodes based on its central premise of the cattle drive as the Odyssey. The story concerns Tom Dunson (John Wayne), a man who yearns to start his own ranch, and, for this reason, leaves a wagon train on its journey west, a decision that involves his saying farewell to his girl, Fen (Colleen Gary). With his friend, Groot (played by the cantankerous, and glorious, Walter Brennan), and a solitary bull, Tom heads out alone, only to discover after he is attacked by Indians that the members of the wagon train, and Fen, have been slaughtered by the same band. The next day, the two men come across a boy, Matthew Garth, babbling of fire and smoke and trailing a lone cow, and they invite him to tag along. When, finally, they reach a stretch of land that will become home to the dream cattle ranch, it's clear that the two animals will be the Adam and Eve of the herd. The older man, however, makes it clear to Matt that the ranch brand – the Red River D, for Dunson – will not include the boy's M until the lad has earned it.

Fourteen years pass. Now, Tom is older (that is, the Duke has dusted his hair unconvincingly with some flour), and Matt has grown into full loveliness as Montgomery Clift, complete with wide-brimmed stetson and a gun belt hanging provocatively round his hips. At the same time, the ranch has grown from one bull and a cow to a mighty herd, but the Civil War has been and gone, and Texas cattle prices have plummeted. As Tom sees it, the only solution to this economic crisis is to take the herd to market in Missouri through country that is crawling with bandits and Indians. 'Take 'em to Missouri, Matt,' he commands, and so a strenuous journey begins, so strenuous that, in time, Tom starts to crack; he becomes cruel and tyrannical with his men, including Matt and Groot; the cattle drive rumbles with mutiny. Finally, when Tom threatens to lynch two men who have tried to run away, Matt rebels and confiscates the herd. He intends to follow another route, along the Chisholm Trail to Abilene in Kansas, which seems to be a safer bet, but is little more than a traveller's tale. Enraged, Tom vows to kill Matt some day, and he heads back to base to raise a team that will help him do just that.

Thus, the original story of a quest takes on the added impetus of a chase; Matt, if not afraid of Tom, knows that the older man has a rigidity of purpose and that he will pursue him as long as he has the strength. The trail continues towards its new destination, and then, rather late in the day for some 1948 reviewers, a woman, a second woman, enters the story.

This happens when Matt and his team rescue a wagon train from a group of marauding Indians; the young man falls for Tess Millay (Joanne Dru), although he doesn't allow her to join him on his journey. She does join Tom, however, when he, in turn, comes across the wagon train, and so she is able to ride ahead to Abilene and warn Matt that his nemesis is on the way. The film ends, not with the triumph of delivering the cattle to market, as one might expect, or with a boy and girl coming together, but with a showdown between the two men. Not that 'showdown' indicates the true substance of the scene. Tom shoots at Matt; Matt refuses to draw; Tom accuses the renegade of being soft; Matt ignores him. The two end up in a fist fight, which is interrupted by Tess, who tells them to stop. Laughing, and forgiving, Tom indicates that Matt has earned his own initial next to the Red River D. The story winds up with renewed comradeship, and the suggestion that the lovers will be married.

It can be seen from this summary that *Red River* may look like a standard western, but that it follows its own, highly personal, contours. Gerald Mast points out, in his extensive study of Hawks, that it's as much a psychological study as an action adventure. (Action is often promised, for example, but never happens: Matt's prowess with the gun is clearly established, but the expected confrontation with one of the team fails to materialise.) Mast also points out that, as with all Hawks' best films, the story is carefully shaped, with early scenes setting up echoes that are amplified later on, and with imagery, he implies, that carries meaning concisely, like a poem. These techniques are crucial to the film's gay possibilities, and to Clift's contribution to them.

The most important question is the precise nature of the relationship between the two men, and here one has to be very careful about descriptions that are really interpretations. For example, blurbs on the back of video boxes, plot summaries on web sites, even the great McCann himself, refer to Matt as Tom's adopted son. On the face of it, this seems self-evident: there is an age difference (at the time of filming Clift was twenty-six), and Wayne was supposed to be fifty. Yet, as we shall see, the film only offers that definition late in the day, and in circumstances that make it a less containing label than it might at first appear. Forget 'father' and 'son': Tom and Matt are two guys, bound emotionally by deep affection, as a number of early scenes make clear, and by the memory of the slaughtered wagon train; they are linked, too, by a common enterprise, the Red River herd. An intensity in love and work suggests a more complex bond than the joshing buddy relationship of, say, *Butch Cassidy and the Sundance Kid* (1969). Another important aspect of this intensity lies, not in the characters as individuals, but in their structural function within the film. Like many Hollywood professionals, then and now, Hawks conceived his shows as stories about pairing. (He mainly operated as his own producer; many of his scripts display similar concerns, never mind who is supposed to have written them.) He was particularly fond of taking an established figure, such as Humphrey Bogart in *To Have and Have Not* (1944), or Wayne in *Red River*, and teaming him with a newcomer, often a woman; there was a Pygmalion element to his nature. Most famously, he used the very young Lauren Bacall to swap sexy badinage with the much older Humphrey Bogart; in this way, he stimulated the audience's interest in how old would blend with new, how the pair could move towards love, and therefore bring their different personalities into balance. It's a kind of adolescent game of contrasts that plays with different textures and human styles, in a half-humorous, half-flirtatious fashion. On a crude level, Clift can be seen as the Hawksian 'girl'; like Bacall, he was new to cinema audiences, and he was placed opposite the more established figure of Wayne at the centre of the film's interest. Yet the analogy goes deeper. Mast has observed how Hawks perceived stars as something more than just people on a screen; their way of moving and speaking was a vital element in the very meaning of the films. This approach is clear in the Clift-Wayne pairing. For example, notice how both move, Clift's delicacy contrasting with Wayne's rougher, but equally eloquent, form of dance. Also, their voices are like two complementary notes in a chord; it's significant that both use hesitation to convey thought and deeper meanings in the dialogue; Duke speaks in his gravely drawl; Clift's tones are higher and younger. On the surface, therefore, they may appear to be different, but the film is encouraging us to notice underlying harmonies. What might be called Hawks' romance of texture is clearly in play.

Sensing this romance, the gay viewer is justified in thinking that an implied love story may be on offer. All the same, romance isn't quite the same as love, and *Red River* would remain an attractive, but uninteresting, film if it dealt with an affectionate male pairing and nothing more. Yet there is another structural element in the story, running through it like a subterranean stream, which contains other, more passionate possibilities. For this open-air western, with its sweeping landscape and thundering herds, is also an interior drama contained within the subsidiary story of a modest snake's head bracelet.

This story (it's a mini-*Odyssey* in itself) begins in the opening minutes of the film, and, at first, appears to be nothing more than a prop designed to establish a one-off plot point. When Tom says farewell to Fen, he places this object round her wrist; it's a token, we infer, of what he feels. It appears again, in another significant close up, when Tom and Groot have beaten off the Indians' night time raid: Tom has killed one of their number, and he finds the bracelet round the corpse's wrist; viewers know full well the death that it signifies. That seems to be that, but then, in Clift's first scene as the adult Matt, it's glimpsed briefly on his wrist when he lights Wayne's cigarette. Later, however, much later, it crops up again. Now we are well on in the film: Matt has met Tess and left her, and Tom, in pursuit, has caught up with the wagon train. There follows a scene in Tess's tent where she and the older man discuss her relationship with Matt. Suddenly, out of the blue, Tom sees the bracelet on her wrist; it's a love sign. 'How did you get that away from him?' he growls, suggesting that the bauble has come to represent a change in the young man's allegiance. In the overall structure of the film, this reappearance is a surprise. It's odd, in what is supposed to be an action epic, to find a mere trinket popping up again, and carrying such a weight of unarticulated emotion.

At this point, gay admirers of Hawks start to feel their antennas twitching; we are familiar with the way this director uses concrete objects to contain less definable feelings and to hold them within the film. Hawks' work rarely wears its heart on its sleeve; emotions are often not spoken, but acted out in rituals that involve symbolic, yet real, things. One of the most common instances is the sharing of cigarettes. Bogie and Bacall light each other's in *The Big Sleep* (1946); John Wayne and Dean Martin have a mutual tobacco-and-paper rolling thing in another western, *Rio Bravo* (1959); Clift and the Duke are at it in this film, too. In a cinematic world that is reluctant to voice feeling, the concrete contains the intangible. This means that the snake's head bracelet is the vehicle of love.

What kind of love, though? The bracelet is significant only because it brings into focus wider issues that have been running throughout the film. This isn't a matter of plot, but of the thread of feeling running through it. Before we trace the thread, it's worth mentioning, briefly, how a film's technique can mould that feeling.

Put baldly, it's all in the cutting: our reaction to a shot is shaped by the ones immediately surrounding it. For instance, the hero smiles, then we see the heroine smile; as viewers, we read meaning through the relationshipbetween the two images. The same applies in the wider context of scenes. Think of the early Universal horror films, where the nightmare of the stormy night, which has seen the creation of Frankenstein's monster, is contrasted with the calm morning that follows: we feel the relief, but the sense of re-established normality is undermined by our awareness of the abnormality that has been injected into its heart. In short, a film influences us though juxtapositions, and, by this method, creates an echo chamber of the emotions in which the response created by one scene can modify the viewer's feelings about another. It's a form of linguistic magic, of rhyming. This rhyme is crucial to *Red River*'s thread of feeling, especially to the relationship between Matt and Tom.

Back we go to the early sequences. Tom's farewell to Fen establishes one clear note, that of the abandoning of love. When he realises that his girl is dead, the expression on his face indicates anger, and shock. In the very next scene, the young Matt (played by Mickey Kuhn) enters the story, and he carries with him the emotional echo from the previous scene. Therefore, even though the surface of the sequence is a macho confrontation involving aggression and guns, a memory of tenderness and pain hovers over it; it breathes the air of lost love, and the possibility of love's return. Perhaps it takes more than one viewing to acquire this sense, but it exists subconsciously the first time round. Clift's character, along with the film as a whole, lives within a pattern of feeling that is not conventionally masculine. As far as Tom is concerned, he possesses a potential for love, not just for male affection, but for the strong emotion that the older man felt for the dead woman.

Mast's study of *Red River* is well aware that masculinity is in question, but he interprets it in straight terms. His response is rooted in the idea that Matt and Tom embody two male approaches to the manly job of getting the cattle to market. He notes how Tom is rigid, domineering and harsh with his men, how Matt, by contrast, is flexible and kind, which is why the hands eventually follow him. In Mast's view, the narrative journeys towards a reconciliation and balancing of male forces, represented at the end by the merging of Matt and Tom's initials in the Red River brand. After all, he argues, Tom's bull needed Matt's cow to create the herd in the first place, the suggestion being that men need both 'masculine' and 'feminine' traits in order to be successful chaps. (In Hawks' vision of things, this means successful workers). This is true, but it stops short of questioning the precise nature of love in the film: Mast keeps the men within the orthodox boundaries of maleness, and the feelings stay inside the prescribed box. *Red River* is such an enriching film, however, because, to use management cant, it strives, perhaps in spite of itself, to think, and feel, outside that box. The effort may be tentative; if it weren't, we wouldn't have a Hawks film, or a conventional western. Still, it does struggle and strain. It's best to set aside the impertinent line of thought suggested by Tom's bull inseminating Matt's cow, and to concentrate instead on the two main romance scenes, which come late in the day. Juxtaposition and echoing play their part here, too.

Romance Scene One takes place after Matt and his chums have rescued the wagon train from the marauding Indians, and everyone comes together to pitch camp, so to speak. Hawks, a master of changing moods, shapes and rhythms, sets these scenes at night, in contrast to the daylight battle that has gone before. Now the world is dark, still and foreboding; Matt and his team are nervous, because they know that, somewhere in the gloom, Dunson and his posse are on their tail. In this cocooned world, Tess, who is drawn to Matt, seeks him out in a grove; on the surface, we get a belated wooing scene, the all-too-familiar kind where the characters find out about each other and hence, potentially, themselves. Here it all is: eyes meet, voices whisper, rain begins to fall, Matt lies in the young woman's lap; this is genre business as usual, with the hero, resting from his masculine labours, getting in touch with his feminine side. In this case, though, the rules aren't strictly followed. Although there are some standard Hawksian role reversals, with the girl coming on to the guy and the guy looking up at her as soulfully as Scarlett gazes at Rhett, the most crucial disturbance lies in the dialogue, which isn't about the burgeoning relationship between him and her, as one might expect, but about the emotional crisis between him and Tom. 'You love him, don't you?' Tess says towards the end, and heavens, you think, so he must, given the emphasis of the scene.

Having set this male love-pitch, so to speak, the film sustains and develops it. About a week after Matt and his gang have left, Tom turns up, hot for revenge. There follows the companion piece, Romance Scene Two, the conversation between him and Tess. After the revelation about the bracelet, Tom opens his heart in a way he hasn't done before. He talks about his intention to kill Matt, about love and its pain; all the while, the viewer is remembering how the bracelet is a poetic talisman connecting Tom's feelings for his dead love with the young man who is eluding him. Given this atmosphere, then, it's hardly surprising that this delicately elliptical scene should alight on the question of children. Referring to Matt, Tom says bitterly that 'I thought I had a son; well, I haven't' (this is far more nebulous than making a formal statement about 'adoption'); he goes on to suggest that he and Tess get it together and produce a real one. The offer isn't taken up; in fact, it's not clear, from a strictly plot point of view, why it has been raised. On first viewing, the scene looks as if it's really about affirming Tess's conventional love for Matt. Seen repeatedly, however, it seems more like a duel between two love rivals, one of whom suggests having sex with the other because the true object of desire is unattainable. Think of that relationship in Jean Genet's *Querelle of Brest* (1953), and in Rainer Werner Fassbinder's film adaptation (1982), where a chap wants a man because he can't have his sister. A contrasting emotional transference takes place here.

These two contrasting encounters, taken together, undermine the conventional surfaces of the story, and open up possibilities of new meaning and relationship: Dunson can be seen as loving Matt, not in the usual manly fashion, but in a more fluid, even sensual, way, like, well, like he might love a woman. In this respect, Tess's presence is more a way of articulating and heightening this idea, rather than introducing the traditional love interest. This isn't to suggest that the film is consciously visiting the question of a sexual relationship between the two men, but its language does enable a gay viewer to interpret it that way. For its whole structure – its movement from a cow and a bull to a whole herd, its use of the bracelet as the talisman of love, its construction of Tess as a vessel carrying inarticulate meanings – plays with (though it doesn't undermine) the assumptions and conventions that it appears to be communicating. Even the grand finale supports this view. When Matt and Dunson pause in their climactic fist fight, Tess helps to wind up the proceedings by crying out, 'Anybody with half a mind would know you two love each other.' The two men agree, although Tom makes a joking comment about Matt marrying the woman. Then he draws the new diagram in the dirt, a gesture that integrates Matt's initial into the Red River brand. This symbolic gesture makes one wonder what the lives of the three main protagonists are going to be like after the credits have rolled. Thank goodness Hawks never made a sequel. It might have been called *Red River II: The Ménage-à-Trois Years*.

At this juncture, while outraged John Wayne fans wonder where they can engage the services of a professional hit man, it should be said that all this has been an interpretation, a personal one, perhaps; it's not the laying down of an eternal truth. It's been offered, though, to illustrate how, at the very beginning of his film career, Montgomery Clift was moulded by film language into a star who embodied the questioning of particular orthodoxies; the echo of that feeling, like the echo of Fen, has been reverberating ever since. Still, this isn't the whole story. For Clift's magic might be called moral as well as sexual; his screen presence suggests the wider need for personal integrity and strength in the face of the competing pressures that can be placed on an individual. It's a complex idea, and it's most effectively seen in *From Here to Eternity*, an adaptation of the best-selling novel by James Jones.

★

Once again, for Saturday afternoon puritans, here comes a plot. Not long before the bombing of Pearl Harbour, Private Robert E. Lee Prewitt turns up at Schofield Barracks in Oahu, Hawaii. 'Prew', a fine company bugler, has left his previous outfit because he has been passed over for promotion, and is now preparing to start a new life under the jaundiced eye of Sergeant Milton Warden (Burt Lancaster). As luck would have it, Private Angelo Maggio (Frank Sinatra), an old chum, happens to be in the same barracks, and the two soon become inseparable opposites, the newcomer being tough and absorbed, the Italian American being feisty and open, and liable to get into scrapes. Prew has plenty of these himself, thanks to his own, recalcitrant attitudes. As Warden calls him, he is a 'hardhead': he refuses to play the bugle, for reasons that are never entirely clear, at least to this writer (the novel is vague, too); he declines to box for the company, even though he has a reputation for being first-rate, because, it's revealed, he once blinded a man. This stubbornness is the engine that drives the story forward. For these are lax and corrupt times at Schofield Barracks. Captain Dana Holmes (Philip Oser), a lazy officer with a bored wife (Karen, played by Deborah Kerr), attempts to break Prew's resistance by subjecting him to fatigue duties and other humiliating tasks; meanwhile, our hero falls for Lorene (Donna Reed), a prostitute with social pretensions. Once these relationships have been established, troubles come thick and fast. Maggio falls foul of Sergeant Fatso Judson (Ernest Borgnine), a sadistic brute who runs the army stockade, and everything comes to a head when the plucky little private is banged up by Fats in the stockade and dies from his subsequent mistreatment. Enraged by his friend's death, Prew murders the brute, shacks up with Lorene to avoid detection, and only tries to return to his unit when the Japanese, as part of the fateful raid of 7 December

'HE IS THE EMBODIMENT OF A QUESTION.'
MONTGOMERY CLIFT IN *FROM HERE TO ETERNITY* (1953).

1941, bomb the barracks. Unfortunately, he is shot by the guards in the attempt, thus confirming him in Warden's eyes as a man who will play by no one's rules but his own, and who has suffered in consequence.

Even judging by this cramped summary, it can be seen that the film is a series of carefully-crafted, if schematic, situations and events; like many adaptations of long novels, it suffers from the need to abridge wide-ranging material, to keep things out, rather than to allow relationships and issues to expand within a less cluttered frame. Matters aren't helped by the producers' need to keep within the Production Code; also, the army was providing the real-life Schofield Barracks, and certain criticisms would have jeopardised their cooperation. As a result, *From Here to Eternity* labours under the weight of some heavy limitations. For instance, the stockade's brutality, which is the best part of the novel, is described, not seen; although the film appeared raunchy at the time, with Kerr and Lancaster locked in passionate embrace on a beach, it seems, by modern standards, as erotic as a damp roll on the shingle at Scarborough. Despite these drawbacks, however, the show retains its life and interest, because it emphasises universal issues about relationships, both those between human beings, and between human beings and ideas. Some of these may seem quaint to twenty-first century eyes, but they still create a powerful matrix of tensions and pressures. Clift, as Prewitt, stands at the centre of them all; he is the carrier of meaning and that meaning, finally, contributes to the nature of his achievement.

The overarching negotiation, the problem from which the film draws its energy, is the relationship between individuals and the army. In Prew's case, this seems to be a straightforward opposition of the 'rebel versus the system' variety: Prew refuses to fulfil what his superiors expect of him, and he suffers as a result. More crucially, he is the embodiment of a question. He queries the injustices that the institution is too negligent to solve for itself; he avenges Maggio's death, and his refusal to box or bugle is an implicit criticism of the officer class's venality. These attitudes throw those of the other characters into relief. For example, throughout the film, Warden regards his subordinate with a wild surmise, but it's clear, as the plot develops, that he admires Prew, even though he knows that his defiance will fail: the young man is a mirror, throwing back the sergeant's image of himself. All the same, he isn't merely admiring a brave rebel of the *Cool Hand Luke* (1967) variety. For it's clear that Prew's relationship with the army, unlike Paul Newman's with a rural prison, is a tangled love relationship. As McCann has observed, there is an element of masochism in Prew: he talks about loving the army, but doesn't expect to be loved back; moreover, he is proud of being a 'thirty-year man', a pro dedicated to the very processes and practices that he can't abide. Nevertheless, masochism isn't the whole story. In psychobabble terms, Prew is not re-enacting some primal relationship where rejection and pain are the only outcomes; rather, he is demanding that the institution accepts him on his own terms, and with an equal devotion. In other words, he is committed to the army as a deeply personal, and, in his case, unattainable, ideal. This doomed aspiration sets up echoes that help us to place other characters within a moral framework. Seen in Prew's light, for example, Warden is an honourable man who has compromised his integrity by going along with the more corrupt aspects of the regime. Maggio is sympathetic, too, but, in contrast to Prew, not tough or resolute enough to withstand the institutional onslaught. Ultimately, these pairings, in good old Hollywood fashion, are like covert love stories running, unnamed, throughout the film. Men are defined as lone spirits pitted against, but also defining themselves within, hierarchies and institutions. One aspect of Prew's narrative function is the dramatisation of the difficulties that this idea throws into relief. He is, if you like, a contained tension, walking through the film.

Another aspect is his highlighting of what, in a conventional view, is *From Here to Eternity*'s overriding interest. This is the question of how men and women relate to each other. To be accurate, the problem isn't as broad as that: this is a Cold War film that uses the days before America went into the Second World War as a generalised metaphor of crisis. Conventional romance is, then, less important than the problem of how women support men, or otherwise, when the nation is under threat. Viewed in this context, the story sees women as a damned nuisance. In two of the romantic subplots, or major love plots, depending on one's point of view, Warden's relationship with Karen runs aground because he refuses to apply for promotion to officer class, and she won't carry on with him without that status; Lorene, who is a small-

town dreamer (her real name is Alma), is keen on Prew aspiring to the same
thing, because marriage would then help to erase her past as a prostitute. In
both cases, the men refuse to be dragged down by these feminine wiles; for
them, rank is less important than a self-contained sense of personal integrity.
The film's judgement on these questions is revealed after Pearl Harbour. Now,
Prew is dead; we have seen Warden being terribly brave in rallying the troops:
in the final scene, the women are being shunted on a ship back to the States,
each unknown to the other, but both clutching a sense of what might have
been. As the vessel leaves the harbour, the story seems to give a sigh of relief:
women, at last, are back in their place, out of the male sphere, which, thanks
to the Japanese, is now a martial world where chaps fight the foe. Prew is also
back in his place; as a character who has embodied complex moral problems,
he is very conveniently dead. His killing off, in fact, may be one reason why
Clift's character remains with us long after the film has ended. The viewer
senses that his death is a dodge, that his meaning is greater, and more
eloquent, than the narrative itself is prepared to stomach. (The novel doesn't
suggest this, by the way; even in the hands of the deft Daniel Taradash, film
adaptation can also mean film simplification.)

In structural terms, then, Clift embodies a number of colliding positions. Still,
none of these would be very interesting if Harry Cohn, the head of Columbia
Studios, had hired another actor to play the role, like Aldo Ray, who is said to
have been the original choice. Prew's eloquence comes from the specific
qualities that Clift brings to the role. Those qualities revolve round the nature
of what it means to be a man.

This is not about redefining our old friends 'masculinity' and 'femininity': the
issue is wider; it's about blending 'tenderness' with 'resolution'. In Clift's
hands, Prew manages to balance, and mix, these qualities without self-
consciousness or noisy gear changes; he is an integrated, and hence strong,
human being. For instance, compare a scene with Warden, where Prew is
washing up greasy dishes as part of his fatigue punishment, with the sequence
where he meets Lorene for the first time and indicates his sexual interest with
oblique asides, and some barely concealed aggression towards another soldier.
In narrative terms, these encounters are polar opposites: one is sexual, the

other isn't. Yet the connecting thread, which is relationship in its broadest sense, is grasped by Clift on each occasion, and followed through with equal grace and love. In both cases, in fact, he is serious and reserved: his concentration on the other person is total; as we have seen, he explores these moments, without conveying any wisdom before the fact. As a result, the viewer's conventional assumptions about how men relate to the different sexes melt and liquefy. Being a man, one senses, can be a matter of defining the rules in one's own fashion. It's not exactly an act of rebellion, although it can be interpreted that way, but more an act of realignment, of bending what exists into a subtly different pattern. This goes beyond definitions of gender and sexuality; it takes us to a rarefied plane, without language, where a man isn't defined by the way he conforms to orthodox concepts of being and doing, but by the ease of the conversation that he creates between his sense of himself and the expectations that surround him. It's a vision, in short, an elusive butterfly. In *From Here to Eternity*, Montgomery Clift caught the fugitive with one sweep of his net, but the dream was never to lie under his hand again.

★

As this part of the story has shown, it's useful to detach Clift from the myths that have accumulated around him in an attempt to see his work with fresh eyes. Nevertheless, the last few sentences have indicated how unlocking the door of one cage only leads him along a circuitous route towards another. It's time, then, for this writer to raise his hand and admit cheating. As a theorist like Richard Dyer implies, it's impossible to see a star's work independently from the nature, or the fiction, of his or her biography; all I have done is reworked old material and created a different myth. This is an inevitable process, perhaps, because writing about films is never a clean-cut business. Indeed, I had better admit that there has been another sleight of hand. I have talked about Clift as if he only exists at the very moment of a film being screened. Yet our response to a star is also a product of memory, of assimilation after the experience. What we see, and what we think we have seen, belong to two different spheres.

When I watch Clift, I am sitting both in the cinema and within the pattern of the film's language; it and I engage. Later, however, in my everyday world of emails and anger, the film can break apart in my memory, and the elements that are personally important to me become part of my imaginative life; they are absorbed into the haunted wood of my own dreams and nightmares. It's only a matter of time, in fact, before Montgomery Clift is absorbed into my ongoing, inner film in which Miss Havisham and the High Llama are the night time horror, and Sunny Clift's son becomes the bright, though flawed, morning. It's a curious process, but intensely vivid, like a waking dream. Maybe, two hundred years ago, I would have been made up of more respectable fragments, like Ovid or Virgil (in the original, of course). Still, I am a product of my own time, patched together by films. It's not a very satisfactory way of trying to be human.

Nevertheless, it would be a terrible loss to be deprived of the dream and the nightmare; without the world that only I can see, I would be just another mackintosh at a bus stop. In fact, Clift has widened this interior horizon: to think about him, to pursue him through print, image and my own imagination, has been a way of pinning down my own butterfly, so much so that I suspect the chase has been mutual. While I have been haring after Montgomery Clift, he has sneakily been pursuing me.

Maybe that should read 'the idea that Clift represents has been pursuing me'. G. K. Chesterton, in a preface to *The Pickwick Papers*, touches on this feeling when he argues that there is a kind of writing that envisions itself: 'The last page comes before the first; before his [the writer's] romance has begun, he knows that it has ended well. He sees the wedding before the wooing; he sees the death before the duel. But most of all he sees the colour and character of the whole story prior to any possible events in it.' In this sense, the idea of Clift wedded me before I ever began to woo him, because I have spotted his butterfly in so many films over the last ten years or so. For example, its wings flutter over *My Own Private Idaho* (1991), in the scene where Keanu Reeves and River Phoenix, playing two male prostitutes, are huddled round an outdoor fire and Phoenix speaks, cautiously but intensely, about his love for Keanu. It's there in the early work of Leonardo DiCaprio when he hinted at

'HE EMBODIES AND ENACTS THE DILEMMA.'
MONTGOMERY CLIFT IN *THE DEFECTOR* (1966).

richer, more complex ways of being a man. The butterfly is present, too, in *Memento* (2000), not only because Guy Pearce shares an element of Clift's distanced beauty, but also because the story, which concerns loss of memory, and the form, which consists of fragmented scenes, both speak to me of Clift's battle, as I see it, with a shattered self, and of his attempt, through his art, to mend and transcend.

Looking back, I can see that it's this mutual yearning that brought us both together again round the electronic Buddha: as a star, he has told me how stardom personally fails; as a viewer, I could tell him how viewing is a consolation for the things that don't personally happen. True, there are moments when a cigarette bears a lipstick's traces, and the waiter whistles as the last bar closes. Yet, on the whole, life is not transcendent. It's more like the final scene in *The Heiress*, where love hammers on the door, but isn't answered, because neither party quite knows how to speak its name. That is why Clift is so potent. He embodies and enacts the dilemma, and occasionally fulfils the dream.

In this context, F. Scott Fitzgerald doesn't only offer insights into stardom in *The Great Gatsby; The Last Tycoon* (1941), his final, incomplete novel, is a valuable document, also. Although it concerns the fortunes of a studio mogul rather than a screen god, its narrator's vision of Monroe Stahr is as true for Clift as it is for a real life David O. Selznick or an Irving Thalberg: 'He had flown up very high to see, on wings, when he was young. And while he was up there he had looked on all the kingdoms, with the kind of eyes that stare straight into the sun. Beating his wings tenaciously – finally frantically – and keeping on beating them, he had stayed up there longer than most of us, and then, remembering all he had seen from his great height of how things were, he had settled gradually to earth.' We, who don't fly, offer thanks to Icarus. Still, if Montgomery Clift could return from the shades, what would he say about the flight, and the descent? His ghost stands at my shoulder. It can speak for itself.

'I'm A Scream No One Can Hear'

At first, I saw red; later, the blood turned to a blanket of white, like a movie screen that's never seen a film. In those early, hospitalised days, I couldn't tell what was in my mind, or what was outside it. It took a while for me to figure out I was still here.

The crazy thing is that California, which I'd always hated, brought me back. To begin with, the sun, shining through the blinds in my room, was the only sense I had. A few days on, and I could feel the pillow under my head, the blanket beneath my hand; then came the sounds, the squeaking of heels along a corridor, murmurs, something revving and grinding far away. I was glad to see and hear, but not to feel. When your body, your face I should say, is one great ache, you turn into pain itself. You lie on the crisp sheets and you think, 'I'm a scream no one can hear.'

The nurse was pretty; she rearranged my flowers like a bright bird, with a hop and a flutter. If I put on her uniform, I wondered (and her panties, and those suspenders that peeped from under the hem), would I feel bird-like, too? My mind drifted back to other birds and other perches, high in the treetops of New York. Bessie Mae, what must I look like now?

The doctor was even prettier: Christ, why are they getting so young? He was a pert blond with blue eyes, and, every time he came to see me, he'd become very stern, like he was trying to hide something. Honey, you should have seen her. *When I heard him out in the corridor, his voice was high with that kind of Los Angeles ecstasy, but he was as gruff as Wayne with me. Maybe he was nervous when he met a star. Either that, or he was queer for guys with mugs* turned inside out.

Guests came and went, some MGM creeps; I don't remember, or care. I drifted, numbed, back and forth between drugged waking and drugged sleeping, so soon I didn't know who or what I was. I figure if a stained glass window could feel, it'd be like me then. I was tiny shards of glass held together, waiting for the sun to appear.

My side of the hospital got the sun — when? — it must have been in the middle of morning. Projector beams peeped through the slats, but the palms outside disturbed them, and only isolated patches winked on the walls. Each one had my face, my old one I mean, and all these faces, from all the different times, looked at me like they were a hundred strangers with nothing in common. I looked back, like Ma used to, looking and not seeing. You know the great thing about a movie camera? It always sees, because it's got no choice, and if you listen hard, even if you're killing yourself in the middle of a take, you can hear the film purring through the machine. 'I see,' it whispers, 'I see, and when they take this ribbon out of my guts, and do what they do, everyone else'll see, too.' It's bullshit, of course, but I liked to believe it, you know, the idea you can be the shadow of your own truth....

Just after the war, on East Fifty-fifth, before the madness began, the sun came in the early morning, and I always saw him then, on his front, mouth open like a baby. After the night and the tears, he seemed to dive into sleep like it was a pool, but I could tell the dive exhausted him: in slumber, a paleness came over his face; it washed his skin like the light, and — I don't know if these two things linked up — a soft smell rose from his body; if I kissed his stomach, I breathed a garden. Movies can't show you that smell. If I went to Ma and Pa's, I used to think they'd smell it on my hands and in my hair. But they didn't. There was a girl then, too, just a girl for cocktails and cigarettes. She didn't smell me either. Hell, she was too busy giving me the glad eye to notice anything; one move of my beautiful head, and she looked like she'd pass out. We have dazzled and wandered; we have captured, and now we're here....

'I dreamt about you,' he whispered when he woke. 'We were in this tower, and it had a kind of spiral staircase, and I took your hand and up we went, round and round and round.'

'What was at the top?' I asked, flicking the lock of hair that always fell into his eyes.

'Nothing. We just went up and round. No top.'

'Ah.'

I didn't tell him what I'd dreamt. We were in a castle, on the battlements, and I hit him across the face, and he yelled, and then, when I started punching him on the chest (I was crying now), his wings grew and widened till they threw the battlements into shadow, and we were high over the city before he said, 'I've got to let go of you now,' and that's when I woke up....

The cocktails girl asked, 'What do you really want?'

I gave her what I knew was her favourite look, then I simpered, 'Clothes, I guess, lots. That tailor's place a couple of blocks from here. Have you seen their suits?'

She glowered. 'Don't horse around.'

'Oh, I don't know,' I muttered. 'I'm not...' I paused and sighed. 'I want it all, but I don't know what "all" is.'

Her mouth was hard and her eyes were hopeful. 'You have it all now. But I guess you don't want...'

When you see yourself on screen, you're angry, you know that? It's like someone else is living your life. You think, 'why's it all happening there and not here?' You say to yourself, 'the world's cheated me.'

Yeah, I was taking pills and I was boozing in that hospital; we have our methods, honey, we have our little ways. Dozing, I'd feel angry and cheated too. I became the fabric of that damn car: the steering wheel'd welded itself into the bones of my rib cage, and, if I moved my eyes just a bit, the dials on the dashboard winked and flipped. This prison, I knew, was myself, and I'd yell, but this only made my suspension squeak. Oil bubbled through my veins, and I'd hiss in rage. My doors opened and closed like useless wings.

Then, one day, I was me again. I found myself in a forest of tall firs, wandering through spotlights of sunshine, with needles and leaves silencing my footsteps. There were two snakes in a clearing: hiss, hiss. I kicked them, and there they were, the bird and the angel man, naked, smiling, in my life again after all these years. 'No,' I said, 'now isn't the time,' but they just laughed, like I was a child or something. As their laughter turned into bird song, the angel folded his wings and lay, stomach down, on the leaves, just like we were back in East Fifty-fifth. I knew what I wanted; I lay on him, too. After this, the bird song died, and I smelt his smell, and I felt the stubble under my lips, before her breasts began softly to press on my shoulder blades, and I was at peace, a different kind of prisoner.

Rage died at that moment. The air brushed my face, and, as we flew, three in one, I knew that, this time, I wouldn't fall to earth.

Then the doctor slapped my shoulder.

'Sorry to wake you, Mister Clift, but some journalists are trying to get interviews. I've told them you're in no state to talk, naturally, so I guess they've gone for the time being.' Then the stern look. 'But you might be happy to… Here,' – he fumbled for something in the pockets of his white coat – 'I have this niece – teenage, you know – Union, New Jersey. Do you think you might – ?'

My heart turned to lead; then, as it cracked, black oil oozed and flooded every artery. You know, he could have been Jesus Christ Almighty, but, just then, I'd still have hit him. I wanted to hiss, 'I've seen the sun; I've been there, baby; I could always be there, and you fuck me around with this*?'*

But I couldn't say anything, and you know what I did? The dark liquid gurgled, I knew the one damn thing I ever cared about had vanished forever, but I still took cutey-boy's pen and I scrawled something like an autograph across his dumb note pad. But, listen to me, film writer, with every stroke of the nib I whispered to myself what I tell you now. God damn the movies; God damn it all.

Notes & Sources

Remember that song in *The Sound of Music* (1965): 'Nothing comes from nothing'? As a general rule, books about Montgomery Clift are inadequately sourced; it's difficult to work out where things came from, and most crucially, in what context they originally appeared. This section aims, therefore, to tell the reader the where and the why of the material, and, now and then, to offer up a few thoughts on issues that may be tangential to the main story, but are none the less worth mentioning. As footnotes are so much pebbledash, and bibliographies not very enlightening lists, I offer instead a brief chapter-by-chapter chronicle, each segment ending with full details of the material relevant to it, and divided into sub-headings for ease of reference. With luck, this method will provide handy one-stop shopping for readers who like to know about sources, or, indeed, feel the need for some schoolmasterly 'further reading'.

All editions are the ones I used; they are not necessarily the first edition, and film scholars will, no doubt, wince at the sins of omission and commission. Film dates are those of the first release.

'God Bless the Sunday Matinée'

For convenience, all the main biographies about, or featuring Clift, are listed below, although they are used throughout. Bosworth and LaGuardia have been discussed at length already, but it's worth mentioning that Barney Hoskyns' is a lively extended essay, glimmering with excellent photographs, although one wishes that he had had more space to develop some potentially interesting insights. Maurice Leonard's book is valuable only for its opening chapters on his fling with the star, and John Parker's compendium biography is louche fun, and that is about it. I note some web sites, too, because they reveal how the myth is alive and kicking, unrevised, in cyber space.

'Love in a dark time' is a wonderful phrase, but, unfortunately, it isn't mine; it's the title of Colm Toibin's book of essays on gay artists. See the notes to *The Elusive Butterfly* chapter.

Biographies about or featuring Montgomery Clift

Bosworth, Patricia, *Montgomery Clift: A Biography*, Harcourt Brace Jovanovich, New York, 1978.
Hoskyns, Barney, *Montgomery Clift: Beautiful Loser*, Bloomsbury, London, 1991.
LaGuardia, Robert, *Monty: A Biography of Montgomery Clift*, Arbor House, New York, 1977.
Leonard, Maurice, *Montgomery Clift*, Hodder & Stoughton, London, 1997.
Parker, Jim, *Five For Hollywood*, Macmillan, London, 1989.

Web Sites

Crystal's Montgomery Clift Page:
www.angelfire.com/or2/classicstars/clift.html
Montgomery Clift Shrine:
www.montyclift.com
Movie Actors:
www.movieactors.com/50stars/clift.htm
Internet Movies Database:
www uk.imdb.com (general reference)

The Changeling's Son

For the sources, please see above. The spine of this account comes from Bosworth: any unattributed quotation comes from her; other writers are mentioned by name at the appropriate point in the text. I wrote this short account of Clift's life with a heavy heart, because I mistrusted so much of what I was told, and numerous questions remain unanswered. To take just one example: his youthful wanderings in Europe are presented in a vacuum; we don't know the precise cultural influence his extended Grand Tour might have had on him. It's significant, perhaps, that in contrast to Dean and Brando, he seems very un-American to these British eyes, and though we are told that he could speak German, someone who clearly couldn't offers the evidence. There are numerous instances of this kind of thing: 'When the legend becomes fact, print the legend.' The famous advice from John Ford's *The Man Who Shot Liberty Valance* (1962) is followed too frequently in film star biographies.

By the way, talking about legend, Clift wasn't 'princess tiny meat'; according to Maurice Leonard, he was averagely endowed, although, by the late 1950s, the endowment didn't always function. 'There's no more oil in the well,' as he complained to his lover.

Books about Elizabeth Taylor
Kelley, Kitty, *Elizabeth Taylor: The Last Star*, Michael Joseph, London, 1981.
Morley, Sheridan, *Elizabeth Taylor*, Pavilion Books, London, 1988.
Spoto, Donald, *Elizabeth Taylor*, Little Brown, London, 1995.
Taylor, Elizabeth, *Elizabeth Taylor: An Informal Memoir*, Harper & Row, New York, 1964.
Waterbury, Ruth, *Elizabeth Taylor*, Robert Hale, London, 1964.

Books about Hollywood and Gayness
McGilligan, Patrick, *George Cukor: A Double Life*, Faber & Faber, London, 1992.
Madsen, Alex, *The Sewing Circle*, Robson, London, 1996.
Russo, Vito, *The Celluloid Closet: Homosexuality in the Movies*, Harper & Row, New York, 1987.

The Vanishing Man

A number of differing sources were used here in order to pin down the contexts that are missing from the standard accounts. Alice Miller is a Freudian revisionist, whose thoughts on childhood, as her title suggests, indicate a new way of looking at Clift's early experience. Gayness as such isn't her concern, but the book is valuable for the light it shines on how a sensitive child can be formed by early experience, and how art is both a way of dealing, and failing to deal, with the trauma. Meryl Storr's collection of essays and book extracts on bisexuality offers stimulating insights and contexts; this is where Fred Klein, Marjorie Garber and Tiresias come from. George Chauncey's book on early gay New York was a stimulus to thinking about gay public language, while Mark Thompson's collection of interviews about the nature of the gay soul may have enough New Age nonsense to make you weep, but it contains, all the same, central questions, and images, which echo throughout this book. Simon Callow's account of acting is the most valuable of its kind that I have ever found; Charles Winecoff's biography of Anthony Perkins is useful contrast material, written from a gay perspective, although a little too keen, perhaps, to trumpet the nightmare of the Hollywood closet, if such a thing ever existed.

Janet Ciriello and Barbara Schave's book on twins is cited, because an instinct told me that Clift being a twin was important, and I still think so, but the evidence is so flimsy that nothing definite can be pinned down. This is true for Clift's background as a whole. For instance, what did he really feel about his father, who is generally painted as a lugubrious nothing hanging around the story? How did Clift's New York (from the 1940s on, he lived around the East Fifties or Sixties till his death) intersect with gay New York, and does this have any significance? Only years of searching would resolve these issues, and even then, so much has been lost forever.

Books about Life, Art and Almost Everything
Callow, Simon, *Being an Actor*, Methuen, London, 1984.
Kalfatovic, Mary C., *Montgomery Clift: A Bio-Bibliography*, Greenwood Press, Westport/London, 1994.
Miller, Alice (trans. Hannum, Hildegarde and Hunter), *Thou Shalt Not Be Aware: Society's Betrayal of the Child*, Pluto Press, London/Sydney, 1985.
Ovid (trans. Melville, A.D.), *Metamorphoses*, Oxford University Press, Oxford, 1986.
Speed, F. Maurice (ed.), *Film Review*, Macdonald, London, 1945.
Storr, Meryl (ed.), *Bisexuality: A Critical Reader*, Routledge, London, 1999.

Thompson, Mark (ed.), *Gay Soul*, Harper San Francisco, San Francisco, 1995.
Winecoff, Charles, *Split Image: The Life of Anthony Perkins*, Plume, New York/London, 1997.

The Elusive Butterfly

This chapter involved a lot of hunting, sifting, comparing and contrasting. Judith M. Kass's book on Clift is well above the average credits–and–quotes package; her introduction is thoughtful, especially in its noting of how Clift often appeared in films about the military or war. This was a clue that helped develop my own thinking. Kalfatovic (see above) is a gold mine of information. Her book lists and summarises all the major press mentions of Clift, from his youngest days to his death; she notes where he lived and when; she traces the reactions to the biographies that had been published up to that time. This meticulous volume saved me a nervous breakdown in a newspaper library, and I shake hands with her in my heart. The gay writer Ethan Mordden's study of Broadway was another godsend.

The other books mentioned, especially Callow's biography of Charles Laughton and Garry O'Connor's work on Alec Guinness and Ralph Richardson, have fed into my thinking on the nature and context of acting, while Philip French, Douglas Gomery and Thomas Schatz gave me the wider picture of the rise and fall of the studio system. Schatz is, in particular, outstanding in the way he relates the nature of a film to its production and business constraints; we who have slaved in the galleys of television hail him as a brother. Graham McCann is mentioned here, because he turns up at the end of the chapter, though he is equally important in the chapter *The Wedding Before the Wooing*. His is a first rate book; he and I disagree only because he is interested in Clift as an exemplum of the cultural issues of the 1950s; in dealing with the star's films, I am more interested in how he speaks to us now.

I could drone on for pages about the relationship between Stanislavski, Lee Strasberg's 'Method', and what all this means as a gay metaphor, but temptations are there to be resisted. See the Russian master's *An Actor Prepares*, along with Elia Kazan's autobiography and the reference books mentioned, if you want to find out more.

There is certainly plenty more that we need to know about the pattern of Clift's career, especially its prosaic, but important, business side. Connie Tuck's article, 'The Monopolist', in the *New Yorker* double edition of 21-28 April, 2003, suggests that, with Lew Wasserman and Jay Kanter on his side, Clift had no logical reason for falling silent in 1953 to 1956. Still, logic doesn't seem to have had much to do with it, and the agency's patience may have ran out, because, after the Freud disaster, the star appears to have been dumped, or so LaGuardia suggests. If the agency's files are available and accessible, another layer to this story might yet be uncovered.

Finally, it seems to me that there isn't enough writing about how stardom breathes the air of much earlier myths about the suffering artist. I cite the material I used on Richard Savage, but it's by no means comprehensive.

Criticism, Clift's Career
Kass, Judith M., *The Films of Montgomery Clift*, Citadel Press, Secaucus, N.J, 1979.
McCann, Graham, *Rebel Males: Clift, Brando and Dean*, Hamish Hamilton, London, 1991.

Books about Actors and Acting
Callow, Simon, *Charles Laughton: A Difficult Actor*, Methuen, London, 1987.
O'Connor, Garry, *Ralph Richardson: An Actor's Life*, Hodder & Stoughton, London, 1982.
O'Connor, Garry, *Alec Guinness: Master of Disguise*, Hodder & Stoughton, London, 1994.
Olivier, Laurence, *Confessions of an Actor*, Weidenfield & Nicolson, London, 1982.
Pickering, David (ed.), *International Dictionary of Theatre 3: Actors, Directors and Designers*, St. James Press, London, 1996.

Books about Broadway and Hollywood
Banham, Martin (ed.), *The Cambridge Guide to World Theatre*, Cambridge University Press, Cambridge, 1988.

French, Philip, *The Movie Moguls*, Weidenfeld & Nicolson, London, 1969.
Gomery, Douglas, *The Hollywood Studio System*, Macmillan, Basingstoke, 1985.
Mordden, Ethan, *The American Theatre*, Oxford University Press, New York, 1981.
Schatz, Thomas, *The Genius of the System: Hollywood Filmmaking in the Studio Era*, Simon and Schuster, London/New York 1989.
Thomson, Peter and Salgado, Gamini, *The Everyman Companion to the Theatre*, J. M. Dent, London, 1985.

Plays

Chekov, Anton (trans. Ven, Elisaveta), *Plays,* Penguin, Harmondsworth, 1968 (includes The Seagull).
Hellman, Lillian, *The Collected Plays*, Macmillan, London, 1972 (includes The Searching Wind).
Sherwood, Robert E., *There Shall Be No Night*, Scribner's, New York, 1940.
Wilder, Thornton, *Three Plays*, Harper & Row, New York, 1957 (includes Our Town and The Skin of Our Teeth).

Books about, or featuring, the 'Method' and Stanislavsky

Kazan, Elia, *A Life*, Andre Deutsch, London, 1988
Lewis, Robert, *Slings and Arrows*, Stein & Day, New York 1984.
Stanislavsky, Constantin (trans. Hapgood, Elizabeth Reynolds), *An Actor Prepares*, Geoffrey Bles, London, 1937.

Books featuring the Plight of the American Twentieth-Century Artist

Fitzgerald, F. Scott (ed. Wilson, Edmund), *The Crack-Up,* New Directions, New York, 1945.
Meyers, Jeffrey, *Edmund Wilson: A Biography*, Houghton Mifflin, Boston, 1995.
Wilson, Edmund, *The Wound and the Bow: Seven Studies in Literature*, Houghton Mifflin, Cambridge, Mass., 1941.
Wilson, Edmund, *The Shores of Light: A Literary Chronicle of the Twenties and Thirties*, W. H. Allen, London, 1952.

Books about Richard Savage

Johnson, Samuel (ed. Tracy, Clarence), *An Account of the Life of Mr. Richard Savage*, Clarendon Press, Oxford, 1971 (first published 1744).

Rogers, Pat, *Grub Street: Studies in a Subculture*, Methuen, London, 1972.
Other
Barbas, Samantha, *Movie Crazy: Fans, Stars and the Cult of Celebrity*, Palgrave, New York/Basingstoke, 2001.

The Wedding Before the Wooing

Clift's films are mentioned at the end of this section; see Kalfatovic for more details and background. I haven't listed other films cited in the main text, because the information there is adequate for anyone wanting to dig them up. As for print and paper, Richard Dyer's book on stars is a major theoretical book, served up with lashings of jargon, and it's designed to present the issues, not to resolve them. Still, it's stimulated and helped me more than I can say. By contrast, the late Alexander Walker was a talented journalist: his stardom book is a lively romp with Gable, Garbo, Eastwood and company, and a valuable, clear guide to the development of the star system, as is Richard Schickel's study of Douglas Fairbanks. Other books on stars are mentioned here because I wanted to fix Clift through contrast; in the text, I have tried to stick to a limited cast list, such as Wayne, Dean and Sinatra. The relevant reading is listed, along with books that have influenced my thinking about the wider questions of how films work. Of these, James Baldwin's has been the most emotionally influential, while Rick Altman's exhausting theoretical study of the musical has sharpened my thinking about many issues of language and meaning. Judith Mayne's book on the lesbian director Dorothy Arzner highlighted the importance of staying alive to the possibilities of meaning inherent in anything from a haircut to a newspaper article. In addition, J. Hoberman's collection of *Village Voice* reviews and articles helped me to understand, and focus, my feelings about films and memory; his own insights are scattered in passing throughout the book. Gerald Mast's study of Howard Hawks is exasperating and exemplary; Todd McCarthy and Joseph McBride vividly convey the quality and outlook of this rather dour figure.

My view of 1950s films as a kind of generalised closet can be challenged; for example, the historian John Bodnar sees them, in political terms, as an arena in which different aspirations and dreams are slugging it out, with no one view dominating. I mention this, because my view is fundamentally a personal, and gay, response; Bodnar's point is intellectual and persuasive on its own level. Still, when in doubt, I work on the Obi-Wan Kenobi principle of trusting my feelings.

Books about Stars and Stardom
Dyer, Richard, *Stars*, BFI Publishing, London, 1979.
Walker, Alexander, *Stardom: The Hollywood Phenomenon*, Michael Joseph, London, 1970.

Books about Frank Sinatra
Levy, Shawn, *Rat Pack Confidential*, Fourth Estate, London, 1998.
Rockwell, John, *Sinatra: An American Classic*, Elm Tree, London, 1984.
Shaw, Arnold, *Sinatra: Retreat of the Romantic*, W. H. Allen, London, 1968.
Taraborrelli, J. Randy, *Sinatra: The Man Behind the Myth*, Mainstream, Edinburgh, 1997.
Wilson, Earl, *Sinatra*, W.H. Allen/Macmillan, New York/London, 1976.

Books about John Wayne
Wills, Garry, *John Wayne: The Politics of Celebrity*, Faber & Faber, London, 1997.
Roberts, Randy and Olson, James S., *John Wayne, American*, Free Press, New York, 1995.

Books about Other Stars
Clarke, Gerald, *Get Happy: The Life of Judy Garland*, Little, Brown, London, 2000.
Crown, Lawrence, *Marilyn at Twentieth Century Fox*, Planet, London, 1987.
Edwards, Anne, *Judy Garland: A Biography*, Constable, London, 1975.
Howlett, John, *James Dean*, Plexus, London 1975.
Manso, Peter, *Brando*, Weidenfeld & Nicolson, London, 1994.
Schickel, Richard, *Douglas Fairbanks: The First Celebrity*, Elm Tree, London, 1976.

Books about Howard Hawks
McBride, Joseph (ed.), *Hawks on Hawks*, Faber & Faber, London, 1996.
McCarthy, Todd, *Howard Hawks: The Grey Fox of Hollywood*, Grove Press,

New York, 1997.

Mast, Gerald, *Howard Hawks, Storyteller*, Oxford University Press, New York/Oxford, 1982.

Schickel, Richard, *The Men Who Made the Movies*, Elm Tree/Hamish Hamilton, London, 1975 (Howard Hawks chapter).

Books about Film Language and Meaning

Altman, Rick, *The American Film Musical*, Indiana University Press, Bloomington, 1987.

Baldwin, James, *The Devil Finds Work*, Michael Joseph, London, 1976.

Boyd-Barrett, Oliver, Newbold Chris and Van den Bulck, Hilda (eds.), *The Media Book*, Arnold, London, 2002.

Hoberman, J., *The Magic Hour: Film at Fin de Siecle*, Temple University Press, Philadelphia, 2003.

Mayne, Judith, *Directed by Dorothy Arzner*, Indiana University Press, Bloomington, 1994.

Other

Bodnar, John, *Blue Collar Hollywood*, John Hopkins University Press, Baltimore, 2003.

Bogdanovich, Peter (ed. Rosenbaum, Jonathan), *This is Orson Welles*, HarperCollins, London, 1993.

Chesterton, G. K., *Criticisms & Appreciations of the Works of Charles Dickens*, J. M. Dent, London, 1992 (first published 1911).

Lambert, Gavin, *On Cukor*, W.H. Allen, London, 1973.

Madsen, Alex, *William Wyler: The Authorised Biography*, W. H. Allen, London, 1974.

Novels

Fitzgerald, F. Scott, *The Great Gatsby*, Penguin, London, 1994 (first published 1925).

Fitzgerald, F. Scott (ed. Wilson, Edmund), *The Last Tycoon*, Penguin, London, 2001 (first published 1941).

James, Henry (ed. Le Fanu, Mark), *Washington Square*, Oxford University Press, Oxford, 1982 (first published 1880).

Jones, James, *From Here to Eternity*, Scribner's, New York, 1951.

McCullers, Carson, *Reflections in a Golden Eye*, Cresset Press, London, 1958 (first published 1941).

West, Nathanael, *Miss Lonelyhearts (and A Cool Million)*, Penguin, Harmondsworth, 1961 (*Miss Lonelyhearts* first published 1933).

The Films of Montgomery Clift
The Search (Zinnemann, USA, 1948).
Red River (Hawks, USA, 1948).
The Heiress (Wyler, USA, 1949).
The Big Lift (Seaton, USA, 1950).
A Place in the Sun (Stevens, USA, 1951).
I Confess (Hitchcock, USA, 1953).
From Here to Eternity (Zinnemann, USA, 1953).
Indiscretion of an American Wife (De Sica, Italy/USA, 1954, USA release only).
Raintree County (Dymytryk, USA, 1957).
The Young Lions (Dymytryk, USA, 1958).
Lonelyhearts (Donehue, USA, 1959).
Suddenly, Last Summer (Mankiewicz, USA, 1959).
Wild River (Kazan, USA, 1960).
The Misfits (Huston, USA, 1961).
Judgement At Nuremberg (Kramer, USA, 1961).
Freud (Huston, USA, 1962).
The Defector (Levy, France/West Germany, 1966).

'I'm A Scream No One Can Hear'

This comes from nowhere, or everywhere, depending on one's point of view; nevertheless, being fiction, it's totally reliable. Under 'Novels', I note a few books that have entered my bloodstream over the years, and whose echoes may sound here. The 'Other' section fulfils the same function, but for the structure, style and approach of the book as a whole.

Novels
Ackroyd, Peter, *The Last Testament of Oscar Wilde*, Hamish Hamilton, London, 1983.

Ackroyd, Peter, *Hawksmoor*, Hamish Hamilton, London, 1985.
Bartlett, Neil, *Ready To Catch Him Should He Fall*, Serpent's Tail, London, 1990.
Bartlett, Neil, *Mr. Clive and Mr. Page*, Serpent's Tail, London, 1996.
Hollinghurst, Alan, *The Swimming Pool Library*, Penguin, London, 1988.

Other

Bartlett, Neil, *Who was that Man: A Present for Mr. Oscar Wilde*, Serpent's Tail, London, 1988.
Connolly, Cyril, *Enemies of Promise*, G. Routledge & Sons, London, 1938.
Mars-Jones, Adam, *Blind Bitter Happiness*, Chatto & Windus, London, 1997.
Rushdie, Salman, *The Wizard of Oz*, BFI Publishing, London,1992.
Thomson, David, *Rosebud: The Story of Orson Welles*, Little, Brown, London, 1996.
Toibin, Colm, *Love in a Dark Time*, Picador, London, 2002.
Woolf, Virginia (ed. Lyon, Mary), *Books and Portraits*, Hogarth Press, London, 1977.

Acknowledgements

This book began with a duck and a drake. The duck was Daffy Duck, about whom I wrote a short web article, and the drake was Nick Drake, an old chum and the editor of this book. He read my Daffy piece, seemed to feel that the writer could tackle something more substantial, and his support and wisdom throughout the process have been invaluable; I have been lucky to have worked with such an old and valued friend. By the way, any mistakes and idiocies are all mine, alas.

Thanks must also go to two colleagues at the Institute of Communications Studies, the University of Leeds. Dr Graham Roberts and Heather Wallis have been remarkably encouraging; the short essays I wrote for their *Key Film Texts* (2002) helped me to fix the style of this effort, and I am grateful for their confidence in an amateur. Professor Robert Fyne is the books editor of *Film & History*; both he, and his wife Jo-Ann, helped this work simply by saying that they liked my stuff. At the risk of burbling on like a tearful Oscar recipient, I thank my friend and colleague Ruth Kelham for, well, aren't you supposed to say something cloying like 'thank you for being you'? The same goes for my loving, and loved, friends, especially Samantha, Mike, Tadeusz and Mira. Finally, without the redoubtable Alice Hughes to type up the first draft from my appalling scrawl, this book simply wouldn't exist.

Above all, my family – Mum, Dad, Maddie and Jon – must be mentioned for their kindness and understanding, and so, too, does this book's second ghost, that of the late Arthur Sale, who, when I was a student, first let me loose on the imagination of America. Doubtless, Arthur is looking down from heaven and shaking his head in dismay at his old pupil's folly.

Picture credits

Page 6 © Paramount / The Kobal Collection
Page 16 © The Kobal Collection
Page 22 © Paramount / The Kobal Collection
Page 58 © Warner Bros / The Kobal Collection
Page 72 © United Artists / The Kobal Collection
Page 82 © Columbia / The Kobal Collection / Lippman, Irving
Page 88 © Warner 7 Arts / The Kobal Collection

All photographs courtesy of the Kobal Collection.

Outlines

Chronicling the lives of some of the most exceptional
gay and lesbian artists of the last century.

Available from all good bookstores or orders directly to Absolute Press.
Send cheques (payable to Absolute Press) or VISA/Mastercard details to:
Absolute Press, Scarborough House, 29 James Street West, Bath BA1 2BT or
phone 01225 316 013 for any further details.